Painting Animals on Rocks

NORTH LIGHT BOOKS

Cincinnati, Ohio

Contents

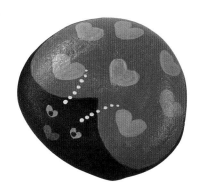

Introduction

Listen to the call of the wild and get painting! Renowned artist Lin Wellford has been dazzling us for years with her beautiful rock creations. Now it's your turn!

Learn Lin's techniques for painting all kinds of animals, including your own pets. There's an entire section just for kids, too! They can paint "rockburgers," cootie bugs and tons of other amazing creatures.

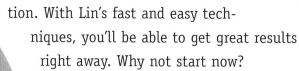

All it takes is a few rocks and some imagination. With Lin's fast and easy techniques, you'll be able to get great results right away. Why not start now?

Painting Zoo Animals
on Rocks

Lin Wellford

NORTH LIGHT BOOKS
CINCINNATI, OHIO
www.artistsnetwork.com

Table of Contents

Introduction

Animals had always intrigued me. Then I married a man who shares my fascination with wildlife. As our kids were growing up, we planned family vacations around adding new zoos to our list, from large and well-known institutions, like the National Zoo in Washington, D.C. and the St. Louis Zoo, to smaller, more intimate regional and local collections like the Dickerson Park Zoo in nearby Springfield, Missouri. What we discovered is that each zoo has its own distinct personality and unique mix of animals. Because the inhabitants are unpredictable, even the same zoo offers a different experience with each visit. My family vividly recalls the time a male ostrich took a shine to one of our daughters and did a wildly animated mating dance just for her. At a zoo in Germany, we watched in amazement as a woman bustled into the glass-windowed primate enclosure where orangutans and gorillas were lying about in total lethargy. At the sight of her, the apes perked up and began to gather at the windows. She proceeded to take items out of a bulging canvas bag and hold them up for her rapt audience.

"These are intelligent animals," she explained to my husband as she slowly displayed each item, turning it over and around. "All day long people come to look at the animals. I bring new things for them to look at, and they are always so excited."

Encounters like these reveal that zoos offer the opportunity not just to look but also to interact with a variety of animals from all over the world in ways that would not otherwise be possible.

This book is a celebration of the diversity and wonder of the animal world. Without zoos and their dedicated keepers and supporters, our exposure to so many animals would be limited to photographs in books and programs on television.

Getting Started

Even if you have never painted before, painting on rocks offers the opportunity to achieve surprisingly realistic results. We live in a dimensional world, so fitting an animal onto an object with a distinct shape is like taking a shortcut to painting success. Unlike traditional flat surfaces, rocks have no background or foreground, and no blank expanse to stymie the beginner. Instead, a rock's compact shape more or less dictates what can go where.

As you develop a feel for how the shape of a rock enhances the illusion of realism, you will find that this art form offers a very natural way to build skills and abilities you may not realize you possess.

Often, fear of failure is the biggest stumbling block people face when it comes to creative activities. It is a relief to realize that not only is it impossible to "ruin" a rock, but that this is a very forgiving medium. If you do something you don't like, simply dampen the paint before it dries and lift away the mistake with a paper towel. Or wait until the problem area is dry and paint over it. There is no such thing as a mistake you can't fix.

Finding Rocks

Before you can begin, though, you need a supply of rocks. It may be helpful to look at the rock shapes used for various projects in this book first. Study the way preliminary sketches were fitted onto certain rocks so that when you begin looking for your own rocks, you will have a clearer idea of shapes and sizes.

The easiest rocks to paint are those that are basically smooth, with edges and angles that have been tumbled and rounded, usually as the result of ocean tides or river currents. I find most of my rocks on the banks of a local creek. On occasion I have bought good painting rocks at rock yards that supply building and landscaping materials. If you live in an area where water-tumbled rocks are not naturally available, buying them is an acceptable option, and you will find the cost is minimal, especially when compared to most art materials.

For some of the projects in this book, I used small pebbles or gravel pieces from my driveway to enhance the rock's shape. Pebbles and gravel are even easier to find than larger rocks.

My rock pile does double duty as a landscaping element!

Drawing or Tracing the Designs

If you are not confident about your drawing abilities, that need not keep you from enjoying rock painting. Many of the project animals can be broken down into elementary geometric shapes. Another option is to trace or scan the design and use a computer or copy machine to enlarge or reduce the image to fit the rock chosen for it. Cut out the design and glue it onto cardstock, then trim slightly inside the lines, creating a reusable template. By cutting out the eye circles and perhaps even the nose, you ensure perfect placement. To use the template, press the template firmly on the rock and trace around the shape.

Ordinary graphite pencils can be used for drawing on many projects. Others require a white-leaded or white charcoal pencil, which can be found at art supply stores, or a soapstone pen, available where sewing supplies are sold. This pen is also used by welders and sold in large hardware and home centers.

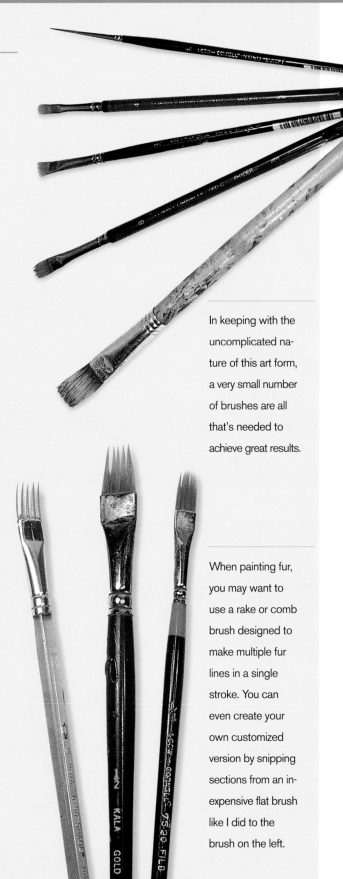

In keeping with the uncomplicated nature of this art form, a very small number of brushes are all that's needed to achieve great results.

Supplies

Brushes

A wide variety of brushes can be used on rocks. Many of my rocks are sandstone and have a surface that is similar to fine sandpaper, so I prefer to use inexpensive stiff, white bristled brushes that I can sometimes find in sets at "dollar" stores or other bargain stores. These are perfect for applying basecoats and scrubbing on paint with a dry brush. Scruffy and worn brushes can be excellent for scrubbing on paint, so don't throw them away until they are worn down to nubs! For fine details and fur lines, my favorite brush is Loew-Cornell's liner in the 7050 series. The no. 0 or no. 1 is long enough to carry a lot of paint but fine enough to make very delicate lines. Loew-Cornell's 7300-C shader in sizes 4 and 6 are also used for some of the projects in this book as is the ⅜ inch (10mm) 7400-C angular shader.

When painting fur, you may want to use a rake or comb brush designed to make multiple fur lines in a single stroke. You can even create your own customized version by snipping sections from an inexpensive flat brush like I did to the brush on the left.

Paints

Any brand of acrylic paint can be used. If you plan to display your rocks outside, DecoArt's Patio Paint brand of acrylic paint is specifically formulated to resist fading and weathering. Because it is designed to use on porous surfaces, it may not adhere as well to extremely hard or smooth rocks. I found that a coat of Kilz, a primer used to prepare surfaces for subsequent painting, creates an excellent basecoat that prevents peeling or flaking that occurs on some rock types.

Other Supplies

Here are a few more basic supplies you'll need for successful rock painting. And other supplies, while not necessary, may make your painting easier and more fun.

To sketch or trace the designs onto your rocks you'll need a regular pencil for light-colored rocks and a white-leaded or white charcoal pencil or soapstone pen for darker rocks. Soapstone pens are available through suppliers of welding materials or at home improvement stores.

To make templates for the patterns in this book, you'll need scissors, tracing paper, cardstock and glue.

A turntable or lazy Susan on which to place your rock makes painting in the round much simpler.

Wood fillers may be used to correct an uneven base or fill in a hole or crack in your rock. You can also use it to make extensions to your rocks like I do to make giraffes. The wood filler I use most is Leech Real Wood Filler.

Cement bond is also used to make the giraffe's neck extension. I use Bond 527 Multi-Purpose Cement in these projects. Combined with the wood filler, the cement bond makes the extension extremely durable. One reason the bond is so secure is that there seems to be a chemical reaction between the two products. Something in the wood filler causes the glue to soften slightly then reset even harder than before.

A clear acrylic spray sealer will enrich your colors and protect the surface of your rocks after you're done painting them.

Patio Paint is formulated for outdoor use and comes in dozens of colors, but my palette is usually limited to a handful of basic colors.

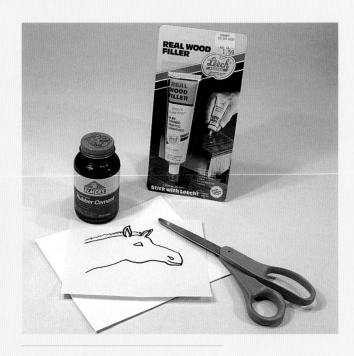

In addition to paints and brushes, a few other supplies will be handy. Wood filler is used to make an even base on your rock. The other supplies above, scissors, tracing paper, cardstock and glue, can be used to make templates. Glue the traced designs to the cardstock, making a sturdy template for repeated use.

Techniques

For most rock painting projects, there are a few simple painting techniques that will help you achieve attractive and realistic results.

Holding the Brush

New painters sometimes aren't sure how best to control the brush to paint fine details and fur. The best way to do this is to hold your brush upright, almost perpendicular to the surface of the rock. Try using your pinkie finger to anchor your hand to the rock as you paint for additional stability and control.

Getting Proper Paint Consistency

Beginners often struggle to get the consistency of their paint right. Usually you will need to add increments of water to your paint to achieve a consistency that allows you to make clear, crisp lines. Water allows the paint to flow smoothly off the tip of the brush bristles. Too much water, however, will make the strokes fade as they dry. Paint that is too thick will clot on the brush, causing broken lines or fuzzy strokes rather than the cleanly defined lines you need. Once the paint is right, you should be able to make at least three or four sets of lines between refills, perhaps many more.

Practicing on newsprint can be a great help. I always lay newspaper on my work surface. It protects my tabletop and also provides the perfect testing surface for checking the consistency of paint for brushstrokes.

Drybrushing

Shadows and highlights are two elements that lend to the realism of the zoo animals in this book. And they're easy to paint with drybrushing. Use a stiff or worn-to-the-nub brush and fairly dry paint to drybrush, or scrub, the pigment into place. Drybrushing yields a soft, diffused look without sharp edges or noticeable brushstrokes.

pressing down too hard
at beginning of stroke

paint too thick or too dry

paint too watery or thin

crisp, distinct lines

Here I've highlighted the rock using drybrushing.
This technique leaves the edges softly diffused.

Painting Fur

Your zoo animals will really come to life when they are painted with lifelike fur. Use a liner brush to paint one hair at a time, or use a rake or comb brush to paint multiple lines at once. Thin the paint as described on page 15 and use the following techniques and suggestions.

Outline With Splinter Strokes: Very short, very thin strokes painted in dense rows are what I refer to as splinter strokes. Use them to define important features while adding furry texture to the piece.

Layer Fur Lines: For large areas of fur, create a row of longer strokes, then move halfway up and make another row that overlaps the first. Successive overlapping layers will create the unbroken look of a realistic coat for your animal.

Cluster Fur Strokes: For a different fur effect, cluster sets of strokes that fan out slightly. Each set remains distinct from those around it. This produces wavy fur.

Follow Fur Growth Guide: Every animal's fur grows in a distinctive way. By following the patterns provided in the projects that show fur growth direction, you will be able to paint fur that is natural and lifelike. Refer to these patterns frequently as you paint the fur.

Use splinter strokes to outline important features like haunches and heads.

Clustering strokes and giving them curved ends will produce wavy fur.

By layering your fur lines, your animal's fur will look full and lifelike.

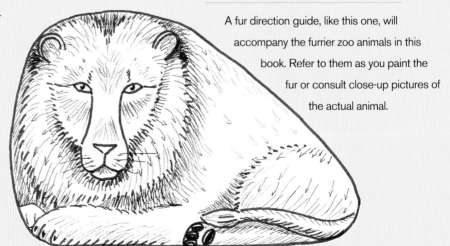

A fur direction guide, like this one, will accompany the furrier zoo animals in this book. Refer to them as you paint the fur or consult close-up pictures of the actual animal.

Tinting Fur

Tinting is a helpful technique for softening or altering fur colors. Like hair dye, a tint is a transparent color brushed over part of the animal. The light areas that are washed over will be tinted by the color; the dark areas will be unaffected. To make a tint, thin the paint with water until it is loose and transparent.

Augmenting Rocks

While rocks already have dimension, augmenting the rock's shape is a dramatic way of achieving even more realism.

Previously, the only way to alter rock was with a chisel and mallet, physically removing rock to get the desired effect. But I discovered an easy and exciting way to change the shapes of my rocks using bits of gravel, glue and wood filler. These additions are surprisingly sturdy and open up a whole new world of creativity. For step-by-step instructions for augmenting rocks, see the giraffe project, page 92.

A thin wash of paint adds a subtle tint to these fur lines.

With some pieces of gravel, glue and wood filler, you can augment a rock to create even more dimension. Here I'm creating a neck for a giraffe.

Getting Inspired

Good photo resources will enhance the quality of your rock painting, so begin collecting pictures of animals that can help you get the most realistic look in your work.

As with all creative activities, practice will help you perfect your techniques. But transforming ordinary rocks into works of art is such a fun and exciting activity that it feels almost magical. You may be amazed at how quickly rock painting transforms you into an artist!

Welcome to the Zoo

Zoos have changed a great deal over the past century as more was learned about animals in the wild. Once our primitive zoos were little more than prison cells where the inmates spent their days restlessly pacing as visitors peered at them through narrow bars. Now much effort is put into creating display areas that are spacious and natural looking. Bars have been replaced by less obvious barriers, and naturalists study wildlife behavior and look for ways to stimulate and enrich the environment for every animal under their care. These changes allow zoo visitors to get a much clearer idea of how different animals live and interact with one another in the wild. Many zoos also serve as breeding facilities devoted to maintaining dwindling populations of endangered species. No longer prisons, our well-run, modern zoos are sanctuaries and havens aiming to ensure that each precious inhabitant is allowed to enjoy a decent quality of life even as they add so much enjoyment to ours.

Big Cat Country

It's hard to imagine a zoo without a lion exhibit. Even when they are relaxed, these animals retain a majestic air that seems to define the term "animal magnetism." The male's flowing mane gives this big cat his distinction, and it can be painted either tawny, dark brown or even black. Though lacking the male's handsome mane, the lioness shares his strong and striking features and bearing. Paint several lions and group them together for maximum effect.

what you'll need

DecoArt Patio Paint in Patio Brick · Wrought Iron Black · Sunflower Yellow · Cloud White · medium stiff-bristled brushes · small and medium flat brushes · no. 0 or no. 1 liner brush · rake or grass comb, optional · soapstone pen or white-leaded pencil · template-making supplies, as listed on page 14, optional · clear acrylic spray sealer

1| Choosing a Rock

To find a suitable rock for this majestic animal, look for one that has a wedge shape, with a flat bottom and a top that angles upward before leveling off to form a broadly rounded top. Make sure there is ample space for the head. All of these rocks would be great lions, and I chose the center rock for this project.

2| Preparing the Surface

Scrub your rock and let it dry, then basecoat the entire visible surface with Patio Brick. A stiff-bristled, flat brush allows quick coverage of the basecoat.

3| Sketch the Design

After the basecoat dries, sketch on the guidelines or use a template as described on page 13, using a soapstone pen or white-leaded pencil. Because the features are made up of mostly geometric shapes, this animal is easy to draw following the steps below and on the opposite page.

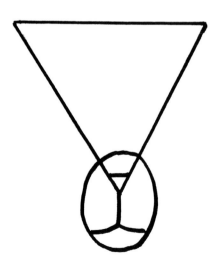

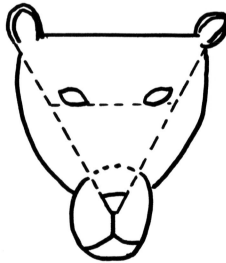

Sketch an inverted triangle just below the top of the rock. The bottom tip of this triangle forms the lion's nose leather. Encircle the nose with an oval that becomes the muzzle and chin. Draw a straight line down and angle two lines out for the mouth.

Evenly bisect the large triangle head shape with a horizontal line. Set two widely spaced almond-shaped eyes on the line that bisects the large triangle.

At the top corners of the head triangle, add two rounded ears. Curve a cheek line down from the lower edge of each ear to join the muzzle oval not quite halfway down.

Gently curve the legs as shown, rather than making them straight across, and give the paws a rounded shape. Here, I'm drawing the design with soapstone; the guidelines show up well but are easy to erase if corrections are needed.

If painting a male lion, draw lines radiating from the head for the mane. Move down to the small end of the rock and sketch in a haunch and a rear foot. Curve the tail around from the end of the rock so that it overlaps the bottom of the haunch. The tip ends above the toes of the rear foot. Add an elongated foreleg that starts just past the tail and ends below the head.

These drawings are patterns as well as fur direction guides. Refer to them as you paint the fur so that your lion's fur will look natural.

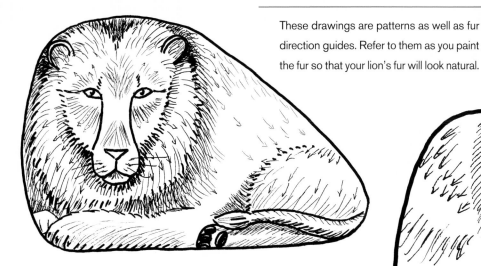

On the backside of the rock make a matching haunch shape with a straight rear leg showing, and a front leg with the paw tucked in to create an elongated oval.

23

4| Establish Contours

Mix just enough black paint into Patio Brick to make a deep chocolate brown. Use a stiff-bristled, medium-sized brush to create the outlines and shadows that will establish the lion's dimension. Begin by filling in the centers of the rounded ear shapes. Surround the lower portion of the head by stroking outward along the guidelines from ear to ear. These short strokes should give the shadows feathered edges. Outline around the haunch on both the front and backside with smooth lines. Make thinner but still bold outlines around the tail and paws.

Move to the outside edges of the mane and darken in the area below the head and around the front paws. Follow the mane, stroking outward to create a feathery look. As you near the ears, narrow the width of the shadows. Work around the ears to the top of the head, curving in to touch the forehead. Then continue around the other side of the head. Finally, paint a triangle above the inverted triangle you drew on the lion's nose.

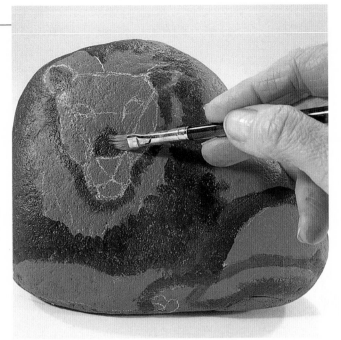

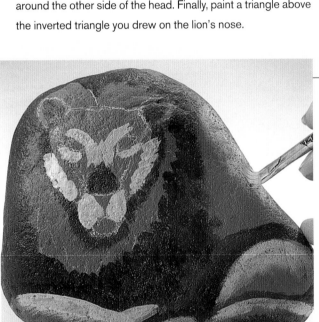

5| Add Soft Highlights

Mix equal parts Sunflower Yellow and white to get a pale golden color. Use a small to medium flat brush to create a partial mask around the eyes. Fill in the crescents between the curving cheek lines and the original triangle shape of the head, feathering the edges slightly where they overlap the face shadows. Also fill in the muzzle on either side of the nose leather, but give these areas smooth edges.

Pick up more paint, then wipe the brush to remove most of the paint from the brush. Drybrush highlights along the tops of the feet, along the top half of both haunches and the top half of the tail. Highlight the top of the lion's back, starting just beyond the shadows behind the head so that a narrow margin of plain basecoat remains. Paint the highlights heaviest along the tops of these areas and gradually diminish as you move downward, producing a diffused look without harsh edges.

6| Paint Dark Details

Switch to a liner brush and mix black with a small amount of Patio Brick to get a very deep brown that's nearly black. Use it to paint in curving toe lines and V-shaped claw tips on the front paws. If there is enough of the rear paw showing, give it three toe pads and a central pad. Next use the tip of your brush to go around the eye shapes. Outline the triangular nose and the lines that define the mouth. Also go around the outside edges of the muzzle to make them stand out.

7| Paint Light Details

Rinse your liner brush then mix one small drop of Sunflower Yellow with three drops of white to get a pale gold clearly lighter than the color used on the highlights. Begin along the tops of the front legs, painting very dense, short fur lines that slant toward the paw along the top edge. Paint another fringe of short fur lines along the lower edge of the paw's dry-brushed highlighting so that the tips of the fur extend slightly beyond it. Check the fur direction chart on page 23 for guidance. Add slanting fur lines to the top of the tail, as well as to the tip. On the front haunch begin at the top of the curve and add strokes to the side of the haunch but stop before reaching the tail. Go back to the top of the haunch and begin to work down, creating layers of fur until the last row extends slightly beyond the dry-brushed highlighting.

8| Use the Rake for the Fur

To more quickly paint the layers of fur, use the rake brush or your customized flat brush (see page 13). They require paint thinned slightly with water. Using these brushes takes some practice, but they can speed up the process considerably. You can also use your liner brush as before.

9| Add Fur to the Back

Paint fur lines along the back to provide texture and to blend the edges of dry-brushed highlights and the edges of shadow, rendering the differences between light and dark areas more subtle.

10| Paint Fur Details on the Face

Use a liner and the lighter pale gold fur color to add short lines to the face. Start with a fringe along the edges of the mask surrounding the eyes. Then outline the rims of the ears with solid lines, and stroke in fur above the top of the forehead to indicate the upper reaches of the mane. Concentrate your lines along the bottom and the top, leaving the center of the forehead plain for now. Bring some fur down the center of the mask to soften the edges of the dark patch above the nose. Extend lines down either side of the nose to join the muzzle, leaving a narrow edge of brown basecoat in place so the muzzle is separate from the rest of the face. Move to the patches along either side of the face and use tiny splinter strokes to give the outside edges texture and to soften the contrast along the inside edges.

11| Detail the Mane and Ruff

Still using the light paint, begin along the outer edges of the lower mane, stroking away from the face with a dense series of defining lines. Move inward with subsequent layers of overlapping strokes, making them sparser as you near the shadowed outlines of the face. Add extra fur lines to the bottom of the mane just above the two paws to suggest a ruff at the chest.

12| Paint the Eyes

Use straight Sunflower Yellow to fill in the eyes, leaving the dark outlines surrounding them in place. Add a touch of Patio Brick to the yellow and give the top half of each eye a half circle of this deeper color. When dry, add black pupils that hang from the top center of the eyes in neatly shaped ovals.

13| Soften the Shadows With Dark Fur Lines

In the same way that lighter fur lines add texture to highlighted areas, dark brown (almost black) lines give shadowed areas texture. Using the liner brush, paint these lines with a mixture of black and a small amount of Patio Brick to get a deep brown shade. Concentrate these dark fur lines all the way around the outside edges of the mane.

14| Detail the Midsection

The area between the lion's mane and the curve of his haunch needs fur texture, too, but it should be lighter than the deep brown just used to set off the mane. Instead, mix equal parts Patio Brick and Sunflower Yellow to get a warm red-gold and use this to add several layers of sparse fur from the outside edges of the mane's shadows to the outside edges of the haunch shadows.

15| Make Adjustments

With the lower mane looking so lush, the upper mane seems out of balance, so I added more layers of pale gold fur to even the two areas out. Learning to use an "artist's eye" will help you see and correct similar imbalances.

16| Add Dark Fur Details to the Face

Mix Patio Brick and black to get a deep brown not quite as dark as that used to detail the shadows. Begin just below the area of plain basecoat in the center of the forehead, stroking up and away from the nose and fanning your strokes out as you move up to fill the area. Then use the tip of your brush to add small sets of short lines just above the eye on either side. These tiny lines add expression to your lion's face.

From there, move to the outside corner of each eye and extend a dark line out to the edge of the face on either side. Next add fur lines to the areas of plain basecoat below the eyes, letting the tips of your strokes extend like a fringe into the light areas along the sides of the face.

17| Add Dark Details Around the Head

Use the same brown color to detail the wedges of plain basecoat still showing where the mane joins the head. Stroke out and away from the shadow lines, using the dark lines to blend the dark areas into the lighter mane.

18| Detail Remaining Areas of Basecoat

Once the head and mane are done, look for other areas where the basecoat remains unfinished. These areas include the lower half of the legs and tail and the lower half of both the haunches. Consult the fur direction guide to ensure your fur is going in the direction it would naturally grow.

19 | Add Fur Details on the Back and Sides

Even though they are not as likely to be noticed, don't neglect the back and sides where additional layers of dark fur create pleasing texture. Scatter dark fur sparsely into the lower reaches of the back's highlighting, then sprinkle more into the middle areas and into the area directly behind the head.

20 | Paint White Details

Use a liner brush and white paint to give the inside of each ear a small cluster of curved fur lines. Add a crescent of white below each eye, underline below the angles of the nose, and paint lines along either side of the center line dividing the muzzle. Fill in the chin with white, using the tip of your brush to give the bottom a delicate fringe of splinter-sized fur that extends slightly into the dark outlines surrounding them.

21 | Add More White Details

Add a bit of water to white paint to ensure it is loose enough to make long strokes that don't skip or become fuzzy. Use the tip of your liner brush to pull three crisp whiskers from the center of the muzzle on either side. Place a tiny dot of white in the upper left edge of the pupil in each eye.

22 | Highlight the Paw Pads

Mix white and black to get light gray. Use it to give the small and large paw pads each a curved line of highlighting.

23 | Tint the Mane

Switch to a small flat brush. Mix a touch of Patio Brick into a drop of Sunflower Yellow and dilute with water. Use this watery mixture to add a tawny layer of transparent color to the middle areas of the mane.

24 | Finish the Muzzle

Return to your liner brush and combine black and Patio Brick to make deep brown. Scribble and dot lines along the muzzle to suggest the hair follicles there, then underline the whiskers to help them stand out and to shave them down if they got too thick.

Allow the paint to dry, then spray the rock with clear acrylic spray sealer to make the colors pop and to protect the paint.

Each lion has its own distinctive look because of the rock that was chosen and slight variations in the painting. The lioness lacks the male's dramatic mane, so adding curving lines along her body suggests rippling musculature that gives her more interest.

More zoo animals to paint

Now that you've created the lion, try your hand at painting these other big cats.

Leopard

To paint a leopard, basecoat with Pinecone Brown. Use Woodland Brown with black added to create contours and shadows. Fill in the head shape with Sunflower Yellow lightened with Cloud White and a touch of Pinecone Brown. Paint the black details and spot pattern. Fill spot centers with the same color used on the head. Use Sunflower Yellow mixed with white to create highlights and fur lines to define the haunch, head, tail and paws.

Cheetah

To paint a cheetah, basecoat as with a tiger, but substitute a spot pattern for the stripes. The distinctive "tear lines" help distinguish this big cat from the leopard.

Tiger

For a tiger, basecoat the rock with Patio Brick. Darken Patio Brick with black to create shadows and contours. Use Cloud White to fill in the chest, muzzle and markings around the eyes. Paint the stripes and markings with black, then use Patio Brick lightened with Sunflower Yellow to add highlights and texture between the stripes. Use Sunflower Yellow lightened with white for more golden areas.

Hippo Haven

Also known as River Horses, these animals may seem ungainly on land, but they

are amazingly graceful and quick in water, and often spend most of their day soak-

ing, just the curve of their broad back, the top of their head and their protruding eyes

visible. While they are considered dangerous in the wild where they are capable of

swamping boats and can dispatch a full-grown crocodile with a single crushing

bite, it's hard to be fearful of them as they waddle about in their zoo environment,

ears and tail flicking almost comically. I am especially fond of baby hippos, small

replicas of their parents but often much livelier.

what you'll need

DecoArt Patio Paint in Wrought Iron Black · Patio Brick ·
Cloud White · Sunflower Yellow · large stiff-bristled brush ·
small, medium and large flats · small and medium round soft
brushes · no. 1 or no. 0 liner brush · white-leaded pencil or
soapstone pen · template-making supplies as listed on page
14, optional · clear acrylic spray sealer

1| Select a Rock

Almost any smooth oval-shaped rock can be transformed into a hippo. The ideal rock is a tall oval with a squared bottom, but rocks that are curved all the way around are much more common. Adding a bit of wood filler can create a stable base. The rock I'll use in this project is on the far right. It has enough height for the legs and feet and the flat base requires no additions.

2| Paint the Basecoat

Mix two parts black with one part Patio Brick and half as much white to get a deep gray with reddish undertones. Use a large stiff-bristled brush to cover the entire visible surface of the rock.

3| Sketch the Design

Once the basecoat is thoroughly dry, draw the design freehand or create a template as described on page 13. A soapstone pen or white-leaded pencil will show up best.

The most dominant features are the large head and muzzle. Place the muzzle oval at the most convex end of the rock. Above it place a second oval, leaving a narrow space between. Connect the two ovals with curved lines. Create a dip in the top of both ovals.

Just above the bottom of the lower oval, bring in a parallel line that makes an upward curve in the center, mirroring the dip above.

Place a round eye socket at either end of the upper oval, and add a leaf-shaped ear above both eyes, slightly indented into the oval. Add two almond-shaped nostrils to the lower oval so that they are even with the inner edge of the eye circles. In the space connecting the two ovals, add two small curved lines parallel to the connecting curves to form the corners of the mouth.

Just above the top dip of the lower oval, sketch a vertical oval that extends up from the dip to between the eyes. From the upper inside curve of each eye, sketch in a broad V shape, and give the top of the upper oval a small indent in the center. Several concentric circles surround the head shape as neck folds.

Once the head and surrounding folds are in place, the rest of this animal's layout is simple. Just behind the outer neck fold, bring down a line to represent the leading edge of the front leg, giving it a slight outward curve as you reach the bottom edge of the rock. Make a second line behind the first, starting behind the head halfway down the rock. Give this back leg line a slight crook to suggest a joint or "elbow," before bringing it down to the bottom of the rock. Place three toes along the bottom, the first just inside the back line, the next in the forward center of the foot and the third slightly past the front leg line.

Move to the back of the rock and sketch in a stocky rear leg with a more pronounced crooked back angle. Fit three toes into the end of the foot. At the rear end give the hippo rounded curves that lead to a straight tail hanging down the center.

Finally, curve a tummy line that begins just above the crook of the front leg and ends just above the center of the back leg's curve.

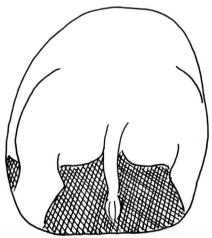

The lines around the folds in these drawings indicate shaded areas. Refer to them again when you're painting the shading.

4| Paint Out the Voids

Use black paint and a small to medium flat brush to fill in the areas around and between the legs. Paint along the lines where they extend into the body at both the front and back edge of the rear legs and the back edge of the front legs.

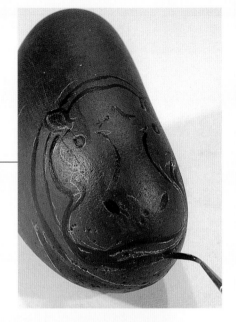

5| Outline Facial Features

Switch to a liner brush and loosen your black paint slightly with water so it flows smoothly from the brush tip. Holding your brush perpendicular to the rock surface, outline the upper head and ears. Fill in the centers of the ears. Outline the nostrils and the eyes. Define the structure of the face by painting over the inverted V between the eyes. Go over the lines for the neck folds. Outline around the muzzle and paint over the mouth line, bringing the ends around the muzzle to curve outward in the space below the eyes as shown.

6| Contour the Body

Return to your small or medium flat brush. Add enough water to black paint to create a semi-transparent wash, and shade all around the head. Skip a space then shadow immediately behind the first encircling fold. Skip another space and shadow around the outside edge of the last neck roll. Move to the back half of the front legs and shadow from the feet up to the shoulder area, leaving a narrow space of basecoat between this shadow and the back edge. Shadow the bottom third of the stomach, again leaving a line of basecoat along the edge. Curve the shadows up at either end to suggest a rotund shape. Shadow the back halves of the rear legs as you did the front legs.

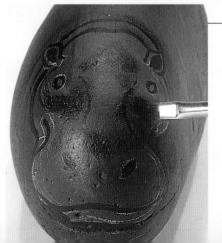

7| Add Contours to the Face

Use the same black wash to soften the inside edges of the inverted V on the forehead. Shadow along the oval above the muzzle and create a wide half-circle beneath the eyes but leave the center of the face plain.

8| Add Highlights

Mix three parts white with one part black to make a light gray, then add a touch of Patio Brick to give the gray a slight pink tone. Use a medium flat or old worn brush to pick up pigment. Wipe away excess paint and scrub on the remaining paint along the top and upper half of the hippo's body. Leave a narrow strip of basecoat uncovered along the top to suggest a spine.

Drybrushing the highlights in large areas like this is likely to produce mottled coverage, which adds desirable texture here.

9| Highlight the Head

Highlight along the top of the head above and to the edges of the inverted V shape. Also highlight the center of the elongated oval in the middle of the face. Add a curved patch below each eye. Switch to a liner brush and moisten the paint enough to create smooth lines. Go around the outsides of the ears and highlight the curves of the mouth lines to make them stand out.

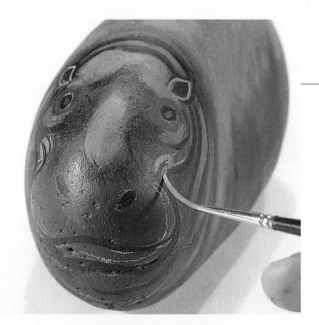

10| Add Soft Pink Touches

Start with a large drop of white paint and add in alternating increments of Sunflower Yellow and Patio Brick until you get a soft pastel pink as shown. Use a small round brush to paint the sockets surrounding the eyes. Highlight along the outside edges of the face below the ear but not quite to the mouth. Highlight the top curve of the mouth just above the gray outline painted earlier. Add this color to a short span of both neck folds just below either ear. In the center of the gray highlights at either side of the forehead, add a touch of this color with a dry brush. Place a small curving swath of highlight beside the gray highlighting down the center of the face. Paint in a solid line along the top of the muzzle. Wipe excess paint from the brush before adding a soft C shape around the top and sides of the nostrils. Finally, fill in the entire lower lip.

11| Add More Highlights on the Body

Use the same pink, but switch to a larger flat brush. Remove all but a trace of paint so that what remains must be applied with brisk scrubbing. Add a light layer of paint along the very top half of the back previously highlighted with gray, again leaving the spine uncovered. Angle your strokes back from the head so that you add both highlights and faint texture.

12| Deepen Flesh Tones

Mix equal parts Sunflower Yellow and Patio Brick plus a trace amount of black to get a darker, rusty colored pink. Again remove excess paint, then scrub along the dark shadows below the inverted V of the forehead and along either side of the highlighted center of the face. Add a swath of color along the contour of the upper curve of the mouth on both sides of the head. Darken the flesh tone folds and the upper curve of the face just below the ears. Finally, lightly fill the muzzle below the nostrils, leaving the center of the muzzle plain.

13| Paint Eye Details

Use Patio Brick lightened with just a touch of Sunflower Yellow to fill in the eye circles. Use a liner brush and go around the edges as needed to create smooth outlines. Switch to plain Patio Brick and add narrow half-circles both above and below the eyes without allowing ends to touch.

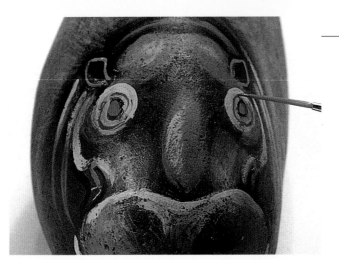

14| Add Dots to Muzzle

While you have Patio Brick on the tip of your liner brush, add a few dots to each side of the muzzle.

15 | Enhance Details With Pale Gray

Mix up four parts white and one part black to make a very light gray. Use the tip of your liner brush to go around the edges of the head, across the top and along the sides of the muzzle, accentuating the figure-eight shape. Go around the outside openings of the nostrils. Sprinkle dots of this pale gray among the dots previously painted on the muzzle.

16 | Detail the Body

Outline around the legs and along the tummy with the light gray. Outline the tail and the rounded rump between the tail and back leg on either side.

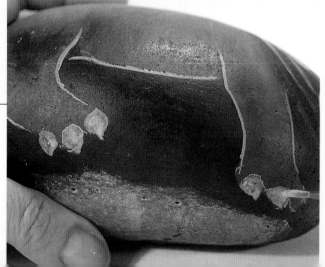

17 | Detail the Neck Folds

Go over the edges of all the neck folds. I added another partial fold to fill in extra space between the last neck fold and the front leg.

18 | Paint the Toenails

Hippos, like elephants, have broad, rounded toenails rather than actual toes. Use a small to medium round brush and the same light gray paint to fill in the toenails for each foot. Make them ovals that come to a point at the tips. Once they are all painted, go back with plain white and give each nail a curved top line of highlighting.

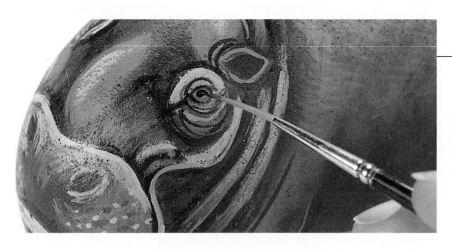

19| Add More Details to the Ears and Eyes

Use a liner brush and black paint to make two thin curving lines like wrinkles above each ear. Paint around the outside edges of the eye sockets. Add thin curved lines to the eyes, both above and below, and add a second thin line below the first one under the eye to emphasize the lines there. Add small pupils to the center of each eye.

20| Add Black Details

Add tiny dots of black to the left side of every gray dot on the muzzle. Use the tip of your liner brush to place sparse, somewhat random sets of tiny lines on the hippo's back and shoulders parallel to the spine.

21| Finish the Body

Use black paint to make sure that the curve of the haunch and the upper halves of the front legs are clearly delineated so that they stand out from the body.

Add white to create a light gray and use it to further define the edges of the front and back legs. Using a liner brush, sprinkle gray texture lines along the midsection of the hippo's sides and flanks. These light lines stand out against the dark hippo skin as the dark lines did against previously highlighted areas.

22| Add Gleam

Add a tiny dot of white in each eye to provide the spark of life. Allow the paint to dry, then spray the rock with clear acrylic spray sealer to make the colors pop and to protect the paint.

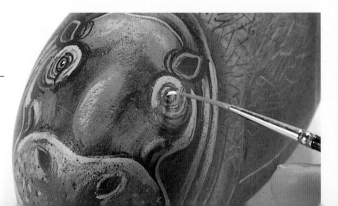

Happy hippos all in a row! The rock on the left was too flat, so I added pieces of gravel for legs. To do this, glue gravel with a flat end to the rock and allow to set. Then use a small amount of wood filler to cover the joints. Filler tends to soften glue temporarily, so apply just enough to cover the cracks first and let it harden before using additional filler to smooth the surface and sculpt splayed feet. The tip of a paintbrush handle can make a good tool for smoothing and shaping filler. Once painted, it's hard to tell the additions from the natural rock.

More zoo animals to paint

Creating a rhinoceros is easy by making a few modifications to the hippo instructions and adding a wood filler horn.

Rhinos

To paint a rhino, start with a light gray basecoat and use heavy lines to suggest the leathery armor-plated skin. Much of the detail, including the eyes, neck folds and toes, is painted similarly to the hippo.

I used wood filler to build up the horns, but bits of angular gravel can also be glued on and blended in with filler.

Polar Bear's Winter Home

The polar bear body is almost sculptural. A streamlined head and relatively bulky hindquarters combine to give them something of a pear shape. Rarely is their coat pure white. Instead, subtle undertones range from the palest of ivory or gray to deep rusty red or golden hues.

I recently watched a polar bear swim laps in a glass-walled tank before an appreciative audience at the Indianapolis Zoo. It was amazing to witness this huge animal swimming with such athletic grace, stopping and turning with perfect precision before launching himself in the opposite direction. It is moments like this that keep me seeking out new zoos whenever I travel.

what you'll need

DecoArt Patio Paint in Pinecone Brown · Wrought Iron Black · Cloud White · Sunflower Yellow, optional · small and large stiff-bristled flat brushes · medium and small round or flat brushes · no. 0 or no. 1 liner brush · customized fur brush, rake or comb brush, optional · pencil · template-making supplies, listed on page 14, optional · clear acrylic spray sealer

1| Select Your Rock

A wide range of rock shapes can be painted as polar bears. A crouching or resting bear with its head turned back in profile is one of the easier poses. With practice you may see other possibilities, like mother/cub combinations, bears standing on all fours or even rearing up on their hind legs. For this project, choose a rock with a flat bottom and a rounded, rather humped top side. Sloping or rounded tops will work and so will rocks with more boxy shapes so long as there are no sharp angles. The rock I chose is on the left, a smooth oval with one slightly smaller end.

2| Paint the Basecoat

Although the basecoat color will be almost completely covered by layers of fur, it sets the tone by providing contrast that allows the lighter fur strokes to stand out. I prefer the look of warmer undertones so I used straight Pinecone Brown. You can make your basecoat solid gray or gray blended with Pinecone Brown or choose a more golden color by mixing Sunflower Yellow and Pinecone Brown. Apply the basecoat with a large stiff-bristled flat brush, covering all but the very bottom of the rock. Let dry.

3| Draw or Transfer the Pattern

Because this pose is relatively simple, you may prefer to sketch on the guidelines freehand. If not, create a template of the head shape, adjusting the size to fit your rock. (See page 13 for template instructions.) My bear's head measures 3 inches (7cm) from nose to the tip of the larger ear, while the entire rock is about 8 inches (20cm) long.

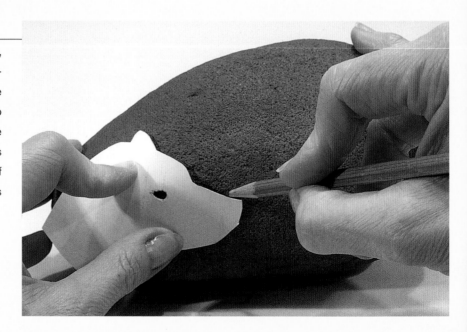

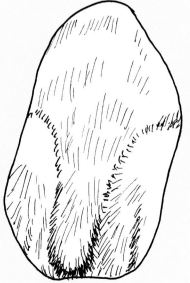

Using these sketches as a guide, add a rounded haunch at the other end that is about the same diameter as the length of the head. Draw an elongated oval foreleg and rounded paw, with the joint or elbow having a right angle that is overlapped by the tip of the bear's muzzle and nose. Extend a rear foot from the lower inside edge of the haunch, and indicate the upper leg with a short vertical line extending into the center of the haunch. Add a rear leg to the backside of the rock as well as a second front paw and foreleg with the upper leg coming up at a right angle.

These drawings also serve as your fur direction guides. Refer to them again when you're painting the fur so that your polar bear's fur will look more natural.

4| Establish Contours

Combine equal parts Pinecone Brown and black to get a dark color that is less harsh than straight black. Use a small, stiff-bristled brush to darken the space between the head and the front paw and foreleg, the space between the front leg and the rear paw, and the triangle of shadow at the crook of the rear paw and haunch. Fill in the center of the near ear and outline around both ears. Outline the shape of the head, using less paint on your brush so that these strokes look soft. Fill in the muzzle area (but not the chin) with the same soft application and run a narrow line up along the center of the muzzle to the forehead.

5| Continue to Paint Contours

Establish the cleft of shadow that defines the upper leg on both the front and back sides. Do the same around the curve of the haunch front and back. Lightly suggest a short curve of shadow in the bear's upper midsection, and add shadows to the area between the tail and the vertical line that define the back of the rear leg. Apply shadows to the same areas on the backside as well. On the front end, darken the space between the two front paws. At the tail end, darken the U-shaped shadow that defines the blunt, stubby tail.

6| Add Fur to the Back

Begin with the same mix of black and Pinecone Brown, then add increments of white until you get a discernably lighter shade of gray. You can apply the undercoat fur with a liner brush, a rake or comb brush, or a small customized flat brush (see page 13). Regardless of which brush is used, loosen the paint with enough water to allow it to go on in smooth, unbroken lines. Begin in the back where your practice strokes will not be as apparent. Paint fur lines heaviest where the tips slightly overlap any shadowed areas, but leave most of the shadowing uncovered. Use the fur directional guide on page 45 for help with placing lines for the most natural look. Paint the haunch and back leg, then fill in the front leg and paw on this side. The fur in the midsection can be looser and less dense.

7 | Add Fur to Front of Bear

On the front side, apply gray fur lines to the haunch first. Paint splinter strokes (dense, closely spaced strokes) around the edges of the haunch and hind leg and on the head and foreleg. Fill in the rest of these areas with similar strokes. Paint fur on the face, following the fur direction guide. Again make the fur on the body less dense.

8 | Paint Layers of White Fur

Use the same brush to apply a full coat of pure white fur lines to the bear. Add water to your paint so that it flows easily off the bristles. Make sets of white fur lines densest in the highlight areas, which are around the outside edge of the rear haunch and the upper edge of the rear foot, along the back side of the upper foreleg and the top of the lower foreleg and paw. Note that I left a hint of dark crease showing at the angle where the upper and lower foreleg meet. I also made a heavy fringe along the back edge of the leg, but was careful to leave a trace of the dark shadowing in place to keep the various elements clearly separate and defined.

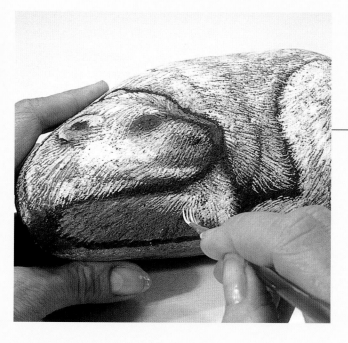

9 | Add White to Front of Bear

Use your liner brush to outline around the edges of the outer ear and to fill in the inner or back ear with solid white. Give the outer ear a fringe of fur along the inner edges. When detailing the head, consult the fur direction guide and apply fur lines so heavily that they are almost solid along the very top of the head and in the jowl area below and between the eye and ear. Also fill in the chin with white fur so that it creates a solid line with a fringed bottom edge. Continue to fill in the areas with fur, tilting your rock to add white fur details to lower areas.

10 | Paint Details With Black

Use pure black and your liner brush to create a row of three curved lines along the tips of the front paws to delineate the toes. Add small triangular claws to the paws between the toe lines. Fill in the eye with black, keeping it small enough to avoid a cartoonish look. Paint a dark line for the mouth and fill in the nose leather.

11 | Create Subtle Shading

Use a soft-bristled flat or round brush to apply tints to give your polar bear a warm, golden tone. I used Pinecone Brown mixed with enough water to make it transparent. You can also tint with a combination of Pinecone Brown and Sunflower Yellow for a more golden tone or, for a cooler tone, mix gray with a touch of Sunflower Yellow. If you aren't sure which you'd prefer, experiment on the backside of the rock, keeping a paper towel handy to pat away excess paint or pick up all the paint.

The key to success is keeping the wash understated while allowing it to deepen and enrich the shadows and recesses of the animal. Avoid applying tints to any of the pure white areas, instead concentrating them beside or behind such areas to increase contrast. Specifically, tint around the edges of the face and head, around the haunch and along the top of the front leg where it is overshadowed by the head shape. Add a swath of tint to the very back of the rear leg behind the crease there. After tints are applied, use your fingertip or the corner of a paper towel to blend or soften any sharp edges.

12| Paint Soft White Highlights

Rinse your brush and dilute white paint with enough water to make the paint semi-transparent. You can test the consistency by making test strokes on newsprint. The paint should be thick enough to whiten the print yet thin enough to easily read the type. Keep a paper towel handy to dab away excess pigment.

Use this white wash to soften the gray undercoat showing between the fur lines in areas that need to be very white. These areas include the tops of the shoulders and along the back between the shadowy creases and the tops of both haunches. If needed, tint the top of the head and the lightest area along the cheek below the eye and running back to just below the ear. If the consistency of your paint is right, you will soften the contrasting gray without covering it completely so that the texture of fur is still visible, while the overall appearance of the animal is noticeably lightened.

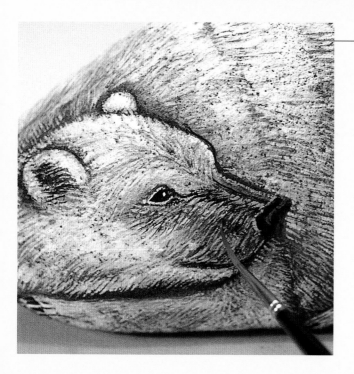

13| Add Fine Details

Use the tip of the liner brush to add a narrow, defining line of white paint along the top line of the muzzle from just behind the nose leather back to the rounded bump on the forehead over the second, unseen eye. Outline the eye just inside the edges, leaving a narrow band of dark around the outside to set it off. Add a gleam to the eye with a dot of white.

Next stroke on a row of very short, slanted lines along the outside edge of the dark line up the center of the muzzle. Make a second row of longer strokes just beyond that row leaving a narrow edge of dark in between. Sprinkle a few more white lines in the center of the muzzle and use a narrow outline to define the top of the mouth line. A narrow line of white around the base of the nose leather will also set it off.

Mix a tiny amount of black into your white paint to get a medium gray and use this to give the nose a soft gleam. With black on the liner brush, paint a line between the rows of fur on the muzzle. Add a row of fur from the eye to the nose leather and a few additional fur lines in the center of the ear and on the muzzle.

14| Add Finishing Touches With Gray

Completing your polar bear at this point is an exercise in spotting both the areas that need a little more dark detail or definition and those that need lighter touches. Begin by mixing white with black to get a deep shade of gray. Add enough water to allow you to make very narrow, crisp lines. With your liner brush, make very spare accents of fur in areas that need rebalancing.

On my rock, the lower half of the haunches became a bit too light when I was white washing. Since this area should be somewhat shadowed, I sprinkled a few dark fur lines around the bottom and along the side a bit back from the edge. I added a few dark lines to the inside crook of the front leg, and a few more along the swath of shadow below the cheek area. On your rock you may see other areas that need retouching or where fur texture has been lost. A few narrow lines will often correct such spots.

15| Add Finishing Touches With White

Continue to rebalance as you switch to white paint, now looking for areas where the white washing could use strengthening. These areas are likely to vary, so it's a chance to develop your "artist's eye" by determining where more white details are needed. On the backside of my rock I added more white fur to the edge along the back of the upper leg and in the center of the mid-section. I gave the tail a fringe of white fur to balance out the brown tint there. The shoulder area behind the head at the far end of the rock is another area that frequently needs more attention. Allow the paint to dry, they spray the rock with clear acrylic sealer to heighten the colors and protect the paint.

Each of these polar bears is posed in a way that best suits the surface. If your rock has a lot of height, try making a mother and cub rock like I did on the right.

More zoo animals to paint

Much of what you learned when painting the polar bear can be applied to these animals as well. Give them a try too!

Black Bear

To paint a black bear, cover the entire rock with a basecoat of black. When dry, use a white-leaded pencil to sketch on the head, the front legs and paws and the back haunches. Use medium to light shades of gray to create fur lines that highlight the tops and sides of the head and the sides of the front legs and the tops of the haunches. Mix Summer Sky Blue with a touch of black and water it down to a wash you can use to blend the edges of the highlights and soften them. Mix Sunflower Yellow with a small amount of white and a touch of black and use this to create a contrasting muzzle area.

Koala

To paint a koala, basecoat the surface in dark brown, and outline the head and legs with black. Paint shades of white and tan splinter strokes around the features and use these same colors to fill out the fur and give the coat its plush, flecked look.

Primate Place

The primate exhibits are always at the top of my list of must-see animals at any zoo. It is intriguing to watch these creatures and to note how closely their gestures and interactions resemble those of humans. The more intelligent the animals, the more interesting they are to observe, and all the great apes offer an endless array of fascinating behaviors. Whether it's the carefree play of youngsters, the social grooming of adults or the calmly astute gaze of the alpha male looking back at me, I come away with a renewed respect for the dignity of these truly magnificent beings.

A young chimp's winsome expression is hard to resist, yet this appealing primate is surprisingly easy to paint and requires only a few colors.

what you'll need

DecoArt Patio Paint in Wrought Iron Black · Cloud White · Patio Brick · Antique Mum · Geranium Red · large, medium and small stiff-bristled flat brushes · small soft round brush · no. 0 or no. 1 liner brush · graphite pencil or soapstone pen · wood filler, optional · template-making supplies, listed on page 14, optional · clear acrylic spray sealer

1| Select a Rock

The best rock for this project has a flat base and an upright shape that tapers to a rounded top. Chimps can be painted in just about any size, but smaller rocks requiring finer details may prove more challenging than larger ones. If your rock will not stand or is wobbly, adding wood filler to an uneven base can correct this.

2| Paint the Basecoat

Mix equal parts white and black to get a medium shade of gray. Add enough Patio Brick to warm up the gray slightly. Use a large stiff-bristled flat brush to cover all the exposed areas of your rock and let dry.

3| Sketch the Design

Chimp rocks come in a variety of sizes and shapes, so it may be easiest to create a template of the head (see page 13 for instructions), enlarging the size as needed. Once the head is positioned and outlined, sketch on the rest of the animal freehand. The most common mistake with this animal is to oversize the head. On my rock the head (as measured from chin to crown) takes up about one-third of the height of the rock.

To sketch the chimp's face on your own, begin with a heart. Draw a circle that intersects the bottom two-thirds of the heart.

Connect the heart and circle with a line for the side of the face. Draw the eyes, nostrils and mouth, keeping them parallel. Add ears.

These drawings are patterns as well as fur direction guides.
Refer to them as you paint so that your chimp's fur will look natural.

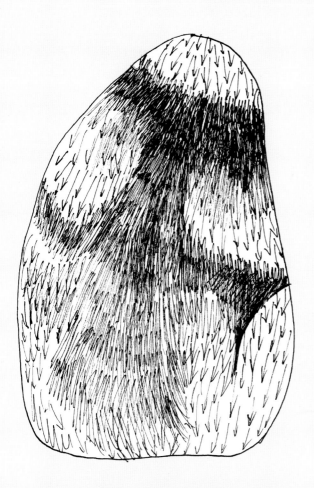

Here I used a regular graphite pencil to sketch the chimp. If your basecoat is darker, you could use a soapstone pen or white-leaded pencil.

4| Paint Shadows to Create Contours

Use a small stiff-bristled brush and black paint to create the illusion of dimension that helps establish the features and makes them stand out. Drybrush along and below the chin with black, extending it down over the chest to the tops of the arms. Paint a dark line around the bottom edges of both arms to define them, and do the same around the drawn-up legs before filling in the space between them, below the hand, with solid black. Also fill in the triangular spaces on the sides where the elbows meet the thighs, and extend a dark curving line at each hip to suggest a crease there. Wipe excess paint from your brush and blend outward from deepest shadows to soften harsh edges.

5| Continue Contours on Back

On the head, surround the ears with a narrower black border that widens like a collar to separate the head and back. Create a wide spine extending from the back of the head toward the base of the rock. Soften this spine line by scrubbing out along the edges with a dry brush. A little less than halfway down from the top of the rock, use straight black paint to suggest a pair of shoulder blades creating solid shadows beneath them in a rounded W-shape. Drop down and echo these curved shadows with a lower set. At the bottom of the rock darken the base from hip to hip. Refer to the fur direction guide on page 55 for placement of these dark areas.

6| Fill in With Peach

Begin with a small puddle of Antique Mum and add tiny increments of Geranium Red until you get a pale peach color. Use a small round brush to paint in the fingers and toes. Remove excess paint from the brush before scrubbing subtle traces along the top line of both forearms. Pick up more paint to fill in the round ear on one side and the teardrop-shaped portion of the other ear. Paint the face, leaving a narrow space separating the muzzle from the upper face. Go carefully around the eye openings and mouth line.

7| Detail the Features

With a liner brush, outline the eyes shapes with black thinned with just enough water to ensure the paint will flow easily off the tip of your brush. Mix a small amount of black into Patio Brick to get a deep brown color and add water to thin in the same way. Because the head is turned, the eyes, nose and mouth should be on parallel planes. Carefully paint in the upper lip, tipping up the ends and making a subtle rise near the right side, where the center would be with the head turned. Make a thicker but shorter lower lip line below. Paint two small, slanted nostrils, centered in the face just below the top of the muzzle. Check for symmetry by holding a pencil even with the eyes, nose and mouth. All three should remain parallel.

8| Contour and Shadow the Skin

Add small amounts of Patio Brick and Geranium Red to the peach to get a deep rusty red color. With the liner, use this to a create a solid half-circle of shadow above each eye that reach midway into the forehead and create the suggestion of a brow above. The inside edge of each half-circle should taper to a point just south of the eye, forming a shallow bridge above the nose. Paint a small V-shaped shadow over the nostrils. Paint a narrow line to define the top of the muzzle and delicate wrinkle lines in the muzzle above the mouth, keeping them soft and subtle.

Make a row of short strokes like hair roots along the border between the forehead and dark crown to softly integrate those two areas. Also shadow the inside of the ear (see detail below) and use this deeper color to add wrinkles and joint lines at the knuckles of the hand and along the toes.

Finally use the tip of your brush to add several delicate half-circles below each eye, fanning them out from the inside corners.

Ear Detail

To create the ear, paint it with peach (step 6). Paint the contours of the ear with a deep rusty red (step 8). Highlight the outer rim and inner curves with Antique Mum (step 10) and outline these edges with a mix of Patio Brick and black (step 11).

9| Paint Fur Layers

Rinse your liner brush and mix a small amount of water into black paint to get a consistency loose enough to create thin yet distinct lines. Hold your brush tip nearly perpendicular to the rock surface and stroke on the fur. Keep the lines sparse enough to allow the basecoat color to show through and even sparser on the arms over the peach color. Stroke on a few fur lines that extend past the wrist but stop well before reaching the tops of the fingers. When painting the head and hairline, it may be helpful to turn the rock around and pull the strokes toward yourself, anchoring the "roots" along the top of the forehead to create a second layer of fringe there. Work around the sides of the face, adding fur to the small wedges formed between the bottoms of the ears and the sides of the muzzle. Keep the fur sparse enough to let the lighter color below show through. Refer to the fur direction guide on page 55 as needed.

10| Detail the Face

Still using the liner brush, fill in the eye circles with Patio Brick darkened slightly with a touch of black. Rinse and paint in two small round pupils with black paint.

Switch to straight Antique Mum to highlight the face. With a dry stubby brush, softly highlight along the forehead just above the brows. Then highlight the upper and lower eyelids with the liner and thinner paint. Lighten the top and sides of the nostrils and the spaces between the red half-circles below the eyes. Add narrow highlights along the wrinkle lines in the muzzle to give them more dimension. Highlight the outside rim and inner curves of the ear as well (part of the ear detail on page 57). Add a fringe of light whiskers to the chin. Emphasize the mouth with a highlight along the top of the upper lip.

11 | Add Final Touches to Face and Hands

Using a dark mix of Patio Brick and black, add a row of short, slanted strokes that indicate two skimpy eyebrows. Add dark lines around the outsides of the upper and lower eyelids to clearly define them. Outline the curves of the ear as well. To warm the eyes, add a narrow half-circle of straight Patio Brick to the bottom curve of each iris.

With black on the liner, stroke on a few very delicate eyelashes, slanting them in the direction the head is turned.

Finish detailing the hand and feet, using a dark mix of Patio Brick and black to emphasize knuckle wrinkles and to add nails to all the fingers and toes.

12 | Finish the Fur

Mix Antique Mum and a small amount of black to get a warm light gray for fur highlights. Add fur lines to the very top of the head and around the face. Paint lines to set off the top curve of the shoulders. Scatter fur lines in the center of the dark chest area to bring this area forward slightly, but leave dark margins in place to keep the chest defined. Highlight the tops of the arms and the edges of the legs as well.

13 | Finish the Eyes

Dot a speck of white into the center of each pupil and watch how your chimp suddenly seems to be staring back at you!

Allow the paint to dry, then spray a light coating of clear acrylic sealer to seal the piece and heighten the colors.

This little chimp's large, bright eyes make him absolutely adorable. He's posed in a way that takes advantage of the roundness of the rock I used.

More zoo animals to paint

Monkeys are absolutely fascinating to watch at the zoo, and they're a lot of fun to paint. Here are a few more ideas for painting primates.

Gorillas

For a gorilla, basecoat the entire visible surface of the rock with solid black. Mix white and black to make gray for the facial features and fur.

Add Tango Blue in small increments to black paint and add water to create a watery wash. Use it to tone down the gray areas, leaving areas of these fur lines uncovered as the strongest highlights.

Orangutans

To paint an orangutan, use black softened with Patio Brick for the basecoat. Layer on fur with combinations of Patio Brick, Sunflower Yellow and Tiger Lily Orange. Use the same skin tones that you mixed for the chimp.

Baboon Pair

To paint these baboons, basecoat with a mix of Patio Brick and black to create a deep brown. Sketch on the mother with a white-leaded pencil. I used wood filler to build up the ears slightly. Tuck the baby below so that it sits no higher than halfway up the rock. Use black paint to deepen the contours and heighten contrasts. With a mixture of white and Sunflower Yellow outline the features with splinter strokes, then layer on the remaining fur. When dry, use a wash of Sunflower Yellow to heighten the golden colors on the shoulders. Darken with a mix of black and Patio Brick and add water to create a wash. Use this wash to soften the fur in the more shadowed areas. Paint the baby's face with a mixture of Sunflower Yellow and white plus a hint of Geranium Red. Add more white for highlights and Patio Brick for shadows.

Golden Lion Tamarin

This small primate is remarkable for its vividly golden coloring as well as its expressive face. Begin by covering the rock with Patio Brick. Once you've sketched on the outlines, use black paint to establish the shadows and contours that give the animal added dimension. Mix Sunshine Yellow with a small amount of Patio Brick and use this golden color to layer on long fur lines until the piece is well covered. Add more yellow to the mix and lighten the tops of the head, arms and tail. Use a mix with more Patio Brick added to lightly sprinkle darker fur along the lower area of these same features. For the face, mix a very pale gray and add a touch of both red and Sunflower Yellow.

Toucan Jungle

Tropical toucans, with their wildly outsized bills and flamboyant coloring, make an exotic addition to any rock zoo. Toucans and their close relatives, the hornbills, come in a rainbow of colorations and beak patterns. Like parrots, they have a compact, nearly neckless shape that makes them fairly easy to fit onto rocks.

what you'll need

DecoArt Patio Paints in Wrought Iron Black · Cloud White · Sunshine Yellow · Tiger Lily Orange · Citrus Green · Tango Blue · Daisy Cream · soapstone pen or regular graphite pencil · small and medium stiff-bristled flat brushes · small and medium soft round and flat brushes · ⅜ inch (10mm) or smaller angular shader brush · no. 0 or no. 1 liner brush · template-making supplies, listed on page 14, optional · wood filler, optional · clear acrylic spray sealer

1| Select a Rock

The best rocks on which to paint a toucan stand up tall on a flat base. They can be leveled to stand by adding wood filler. If your rock has one more angular side, or an area that bows out, consider placing the beak there.

Larger rocks make more dramatic pieces, but the one I chose is a little over 5 inches (13cm) tall with a neatly rounded top and smoothly sloping sides. Though not very tall, the shape of this rock seemed to suggest the flared-out back side of the bird's tail end. It has only a small curve, so making the beak look slightly turned will help show its distinctive shape.

2| Sketch the Design

Use a graphite pencil or soapstone pen to sketch the design or make a template of it as described on page 13. This design must begin with the beak shape because all other elements are dictated by its placement. Not only is the toucan's bill hugely oversized, but the upper beak also has a distinctive curve. To show it, I turned the beak on my bird just slightly to one side so that both the top half and the smaller, straighter bottom half would be visible. Start the beak very near the top of the rock, curving it down toward the base. On this rock the beak measures almost 4 inches (10cm), or four-fifths of the total height of the rock. For taller rocks, the percentage may be slightly less, but you would never want the beak to be less than two-thirds of the rock's height. If your rock has a more pronounced curve than mine does, there may be no need to skew the beak sideways.

The rest of the design consists of the one-piece facemask and connected bib that ends just above the beak tip, the eyes and the two wing shapes. To give your bird a built-in perch, draw in a narrow branch just above the base running sideways until it curves out of sight. Add two bird feet that overlap the branch below the tip of the beak.

Refer to these drawings as you're painting your toucan for guidance on feather direction.

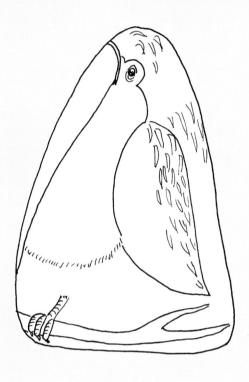

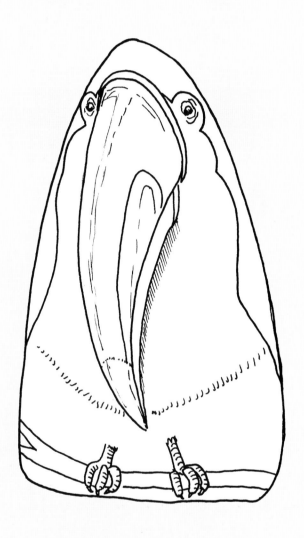

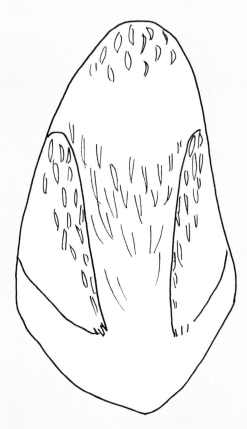

3| Paint the Black Areas

Use a medium, stiff-bristled brush and black to cover the rock, excluding the mask, bib, beak, eyes and the branch. Coverage needs to be solid, so if your rock surface is rough, work the paint into all the nooks and crannies. The contoured edges of the mask and bib should be smooth, but the line along the bottom of the bib should have a bit of texture.

4| Paint the Beak

Rinse your brush well before covering the beak with Citrus Green. Leave a narrow band along the top curve of the beak uncovered for now. A second coat may be needed if your rock is dark. If you are concerned about losing the guideline for the lower beak, simply paint right alongside the line, leaving it uncovered.

5| Paint the Mask and Bib

Use Sunshine Yellow to cover the mask and fill in the bib area, leaving only the eye spaces uncovered. Along the bottom of the bib, feather the tips of your strokes out into the area you left textured earlier. Everywhere else the edges of these yellow areas should be as smooth as possible. If you are painting on a dark or very smooth stone, a second coat of yellow may be necessary.

6| Paint Circles Around the Eyes

Switch to a liner brush and use Citrus Green to create several small concentric circles around each eye. You may need to add a drop of water to help the paint go on smoothly.

7 | Add Highlights to the Beak

Switch to a small or medium round or flat brush to give the beak a streak of Sunshine Yellow highlighting from the top curve down the center of the beak, tapering it off near the tip. Go along the bottom edge of the upper beak with a narrow line of highlighting. Near the top of the upper beak, add a large oval spot with a tapering end.

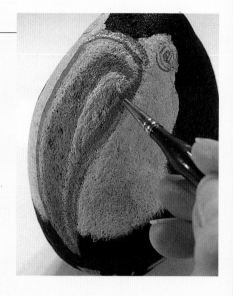

8 | Highlight the Wings and Back

Mix two parts white with one part black and slightly less than one part Tango Blue to make a bluish-gray. Use a medium-sized angular or flat brush to pick up paint, wiping away much of it for drybrushing. Begin at the top of the head, just behind the mask around the eyes, applying a cluster of strokes that fan out backwards. Skip down to the center of the back and add more strokes of highlighting there.

A wide band of black should remain between the back highlights and the tops of the wings, so use a smaller brush to paint in an outline of the wing shapes to clearly establish them. The back highlights can be stroked on in several overlapping layers that reach nearly to the back edge of the rock.

On the wings, concentrate your drybrushed strokes along the top edges, and add several offset rows of strokes to suggest the texture of slanting wing feathers.

9 | Add a Tail

Use the same bluish-gray paint and a liner brush to paint a tail at the very bottom of the back of the bird. The tail is a square shape with an inverted V split in the center.

10 | Paint the Branch

The original color of my rock was close to the pale beige I wanted for the branch that forms the toucan's perch. Make the color by mixing small increments of black into a larger puddle of Daisy Cream. Paint the branch with a small flat brush. Use a liner brush to paint around the feet and between the toes.

Add more black to the mixture and run a line of shadowing just above the bottom edge of the branch.

11| Sharpen the Details

Fill in the two eyes with the tip of your liner brush and black paint.

Paint in the band along the top of the beak solid black, tapering the end on the side the beak is turned toward. On the other side, bring the end down until it's even with the edge of the upper beak. Run a black line down between the upper and lower beaks, starting out heavier but narrowing the line as it goes down. Narrowly outline around the top and bottom edges of the entire beak to make it stand out clearly. At the corner of the band around the top of the beak, extend a small curving line.

12| Detail the Feather Highlights

Use your liner brush and black paint to add narrow layers of long lines that break up the larger gray highlights on the head, back and wings. These fine lines may curve in various directions, but they should follow the overall direction of the highlights. Avoid the very top edge of highlighting to preserve maximum contrast there.

13| Detail the Eyes

Mix a trace amount of black into a drop of Citrus Green and use the resulting greenish-gray color to play up the curves along the bottom halves of the circles surrounding the eyes.

14| Paint the Beak Tip

Mix small increments of black into a small puddle of Tiger Lily Orange to make a rusty brown color. Use your liner brush to fill in the tip of the beak, giving the top a pronounced inward curve. Don't cover up the yellow edges around the beak tip. On the bottom beak, start the brown area a little lower down, curving the top so the inner edge comes up nearly level with that of the top beak.

15| Add Beak Stripes

Use the same rusty brown color to add four small crescents along the bottom edge of the upper beak. Add a longer row of smaller and less curved V-shaped markings to the top line of the lower beak, offsetting them slightly so that they don't line up evenly with the crescents above.

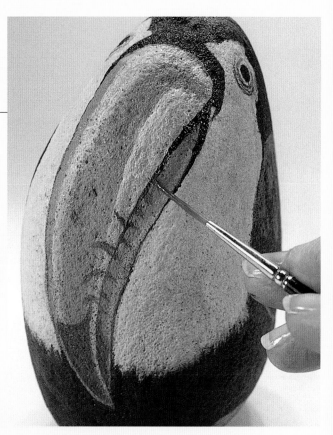

16| Add Dark Fringe

With the same rusty color used on the beak, make a border of short, delicate lines along the bottom edge of the toucan's bib.

17| Shadow Beneath the Beak

A line of shadowing will add to the illusion that the beak is actually standing out from the body. Use a small stiff-bristled flat, adding increments of black paint to a drop of Citrus Green until you have an olive-drab shade of gray-green. Remove excess pigment from the brush and scrub this color along the side of the beak. Make the line of shadow narrow at the top, gradually widening it as you move down to the bottom of the bib.

18| Add Orange Touches

Select a small round or flat brush and use Tiger Lily Orange to brighten the center of the beak's yellow spot, leaving an edge of yellow showing along the top. Paint the edges of the beak tip orange, too. Use either the tip of that same brush or a liner brush to add a row of orange fringe right over the top of the darker fringe along the bottom of the bib.

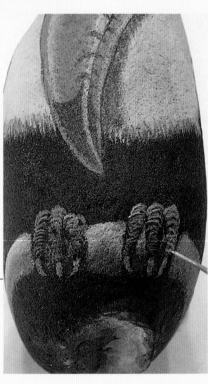

19| Detail the Feet

Mix white with a small amount of black to get a medium gray. Use your liner brush to add a small, curved nail to each toe. Move up from the nail and fill each toe with a row of closely spaced horizontal lines, curving them to indicate dimension. Make these "scaly" lines heavier and closer together toward the top of each toe. Leave black edges in place so the toes remain separate.

20| Add Final Touch

A single dot of white in the center of each eye gives this bird a bright and inquisitive stare.

Allow the paint to dry, then spray the rock with clear acrylic sealer to heighten the colors and protect the paint.

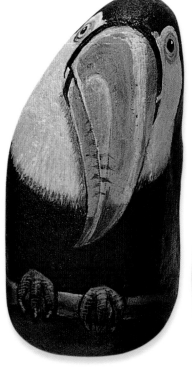

Make a whole flock of these colorful birds to add a tropical flare to any décor! Note how the beak for each of these birds is placed based on the features of the rock it's painted on.

More zoo animals to paint

The feather work on this owl is more like fur compared to the feathers on the toucan. The long, curved feather lines make the owl look fluffy and warm.

Watchful Owl

To paint this owl, begin with a white basecoat, then use Patio Brick darkened with black to add the breast feathers. On the back and sides, use solid deep brown to paint the wings, back and tail feathers. Use straight black to define the shape of the head and the features, then use white to create the delicate patterns on the head and around the neck.

Zebra Plains

The bold contrast of black against white gives the zebra one of the most starkly dramatic color combinations possible. The stripe pattern can be challenging, but once the guidelines are in place, a minimum of fur details makes this zebra a fairly easy animal to paint. Zebras are muscular and compact, built more like sturdy ponies than horses. Once you've mastered this resting pose, you may want to try augmenting your rocks to create a whole herd of these wonderful animals in a variety of lifelike poses.

what you'll need

DecoArt Patio Paint in Cloud White · Wrought Iron Black · Daisy Cream · Patio Brick · Sunflower Yellow · large, stiff-bristled flat brush · small and medium soft flat brushes · small round and small shader brushes · no. 0 or no. 1 liner brush · template-making supplies, listed on page 14, optional · waxed paper and black permanent marker, optional · clear acrylic spray sealer

1 | Select A Rock

Look for a rock with an oval shape and flat bottom. It should be wide enough to suggest the bulk of this sturdy creature and tall enough to fit the head and pricked up ears. If you find a rock with an uneven top that suggests a raised head, that's a plus, but it's not necessary. One slightly squared off end can work well for the chest and neck, but the end for the hindquarters needs to be rounded. For this project I chose the center rock.

2 | Paint the Basecoat

Use a large stiff-bristled flat brush to cover the rock surface with white. Paint down to the base so that no plain rock is visible.

3 | Sketch the Design

Start with positioning the head shape. If you are comfortable with your drawing skills, use the step-by-step guide. Otherwise, create a template from the patterns provided, as described on page 13, adjusting the size to fit your rock. Whichever method you use, the head should be placed as high on the rock as it can go without having the ears curve out of view.

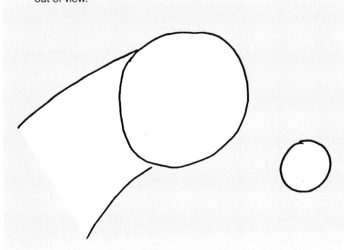

To sketch the zebra head, begin with a large circle for the head and a smaller one for the muzzle. Draw neck lines coming off of the head.

Sketch the ears with their bases inside the circle for the head. Draw the eyes and nostrils, keeping them parallel to the ears.

Once the head is in place, tuck the folded front leg below it near the end of the rock. Add the round back haunch, slightly flattening the inside curve. Sketch in a crooked back leg whose outside edge bisects the bottom of the haunch. Tilting the midsection of the leg up slightly allows you to gracefully angle the ankle joint down to the hoof. Do the same with the back leg on the other side of the rock, and tuck in another folded front leg.

4 | Paint the Shadows

While some animals require dark shadows to establish contours, a zebra, with its stripe pattern, requires a more subtle form of shadowing. Mix small increments of black into a small puddle of Daisy Cream until you get a medium shade of warm gray. Use a small shader or flat brush to pick up paint, and wipe away much of it for drybrushing. Paint the shadows widest along the bottom of the head and neck, along the midsection between the front and rear hooves, and at the angle between the haunch and rear foot. Apply thinner shadows to the lower half of the rear portion of the haunch, along the top of the head, the tops of the haunches and the front legs.

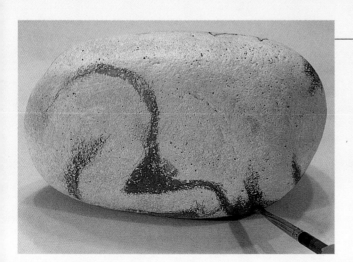

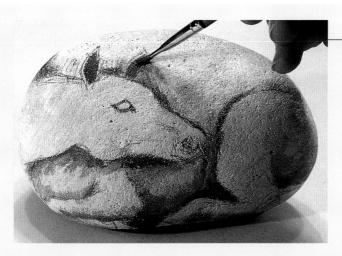

5| Deepen the Shadows

Add enough black to your gray mixture to darken it noticeably. Use a smaller flat or shader brush to pick up the paint, again wiping away any excess. Apply this darker gray in a narrow line to the area where the neck and round jawbone meet and also along the line from jaw to chin. Fill in the angle where the rear leg and haunch meet and the area along the base of the rock between the two hooves. Do the same to the backside of the rock. Finally, fill in the insides of the two ears with this dark gray.

6| Outline the Features

Switch to a liner brush and use black paint thinned slightly with water to define your zebra's features. Outline the eye, fill in the teardrop-shaped nostrils and go over the mouth line. Form an upright, striped mane by painting intermittent clusters between the ears and along the neck, but don't underline the base of these clusters. Go around the ears, head, haunch and legs. Outline the features on the backside as well. Once all the main elements are outlined, use more flowing lines to fill the tail. The tips of these tail strokes should reach nearly to the crook between the leg and haunch.

7| Draw on the Stripe Pattern

There are several zebra species, each with a slightly different look to its stripes. I chose the Grevy's Zebra and noted that even among members of this species there are some variations in the pattern. The stripes on the face and head are the most ornate and complex. If your rock shape dictates that your zebra faces the opposite direction from the one shown, try tracing over the pattern with waxed paper and a black permanent marker, then flip the paper over to see how the reversed pattern should look. Once adjusted to fit the size of your rock, you should be able to trace the stripes on if you prefer not to draw them freehand. Using a sharp pencil, draw two lines and fill in the area in between to draw each stripe. This way, you can vary the width of the stripes.

The stripes on the face start off very narrow at the nose and fan out from there to cover the head, getting both wider and more widely spaced as they go. One exception is the very narrow stripes running from nose to forehead; these tend to stay thin and closely spaced. Note that the stripes sometimes break or fork off at the tips. Such variations give the pattern its pleasing rhythm. A crooked line that goes from the front of the near ear to the jaw line transitions the pattern to more regular stripes along the neck. Take care not to match the stripes up with the clusters in the mane; offsetting them will look more natural.

The spine line begins where the top of the neck meets the end of the rock, then follows the top back edge of the rock across and down to the base of the tail. All the stripes for the body curve off from this central spine line.

In the midsection of the rock, the stripe pattern is again broken by a partial stripe. The stripes change direction at that point, curving in from the opposite direction to fill in the rest of the back.

On the haunches leave a narrow space along the top, making the first wide curved stripe just below it from front to back. Proceed to fill in the haunch with parallel lines that don't quite reach the front curve of the haunch. Give some of these stripes longer curves that sweep downward, and give others forked ends. Where the upper leg overlaps the haunch, break up the stripes so they don't line up evenly, suggesting a difference in the surfaces there. Curving the ends of the lines along the upper leg also suggests rounded contours. The stripes along the lower back leg should be more wedge-shaped and curved as if conforming to the shape of the leg. The tips should not reach the top of the leg.

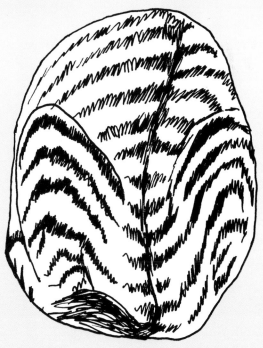

Below the head, the stripes should seem to match up with the one above the head, then curve gracefully around the chest to join the stripes coming in from the other side. Along the very top of the front leg, just under the head, note that the stripes are short curves along the back edge that don't extend all the way across to the top.

It may take some time to figure out how the stripes fit together to make a pleasing whole, but the effort will pay off when you begin painting them.

8| Paint the Stripes

Select a flat brush small enough to maneuver in tight places. Use black paint to fill in the sketched-on stripe pattern. As you paint these stripes, turn your brush sideways often to add a bit of fringe along the edges rather than making them completely smooth. The wider the stripe, the more texture it should have. Begin with the spine line and body stripes, then move on to the back and front haunches. In the picture at left, I started with face stripes but decided it would be better to warm up on the bigger stripes.

Once the main stripes are in, switch to a liner brush to add the more delicate striping pattern to the face and the legs.

9| Paint the Muzzle

On an animal that is mainly black and white, the addition of even understated color has a big impact. Mix Patio Brick with a touch of black to get a deep, reddish brown and use a small round or flat brush with a soft bristle to paint the entire end of the muzzle and chin. Add more black to deepen the brown further, and use it to darken around and between the nostrils, leaving a narrow edge of the lighter brown around the nostrils, the mouth and lower lip.

10| Fill in the Eye

Use the tip of your liner brush and black paint to place a round pupil in the upper center of the eye shape. Mix in Patio Brick to create the same reddish brown first used on the muzzle and create a half-circle around the black pupil. Rinse your brush and make a narrow outline of straight Patio Brick along the very outside edge of the iris to give the eye more depth.

11| Tint the Back

Add a touch of Patio Brick to a small drop of Sunflower Yellow and mix with water until it is semi-transparent. With a medium flat brush, apply this tint in a wide swath between the black stripes on either side of the spine line. Pick up any excess along the edges with a paper towel or tissue. Also add a touch of this tint to the area of the haunch just above the tail but behind the leg crease.

12| Add Details to Face

All that remains are the small details that will bring this piece to life. Mix tiny amounts of Patio Brick and black to make a medium brown, then add an even tinier amount of white paint to lighten the mixture. Use it to underline the eye from corner to corner. I also used this lighter brown to encircle the nostrils, the edge of the upper lip and the curve of the lower lip, giving these features the additional definition they seemed to need.

13| Add White Details

Use the tip of your liner brush to add one or two tiny specks of white to the upper center of the eye and to add a fringe of ear fur sprouting from the inside edges of both ears.

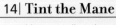

14| Tint the Mane

Use your liner brush to add a trace of Sunflower Yellow to the white sections of the mane.

15| Darken the Roots

Add a touch of Patio Brick to the yellow and use this sparingly to darken just the roots.

16| Detail the Stripes

Use your liner brush and either black or white paint (perhaps both) to add tiny splinter strokes of texture to the wider stripes wherever they seem to be needed. Fringes of fur texture in white can help whittle down a black stripe that got too wide, or to reshape a stripe that doesn't quite seem to fit the pattern. In the same way, black fringes can widen stripes that are too thin or correct a curve.

17| Paint the Hooves

Mix a medium gray to fill in the two hooves showing at the very bottom of the piece.

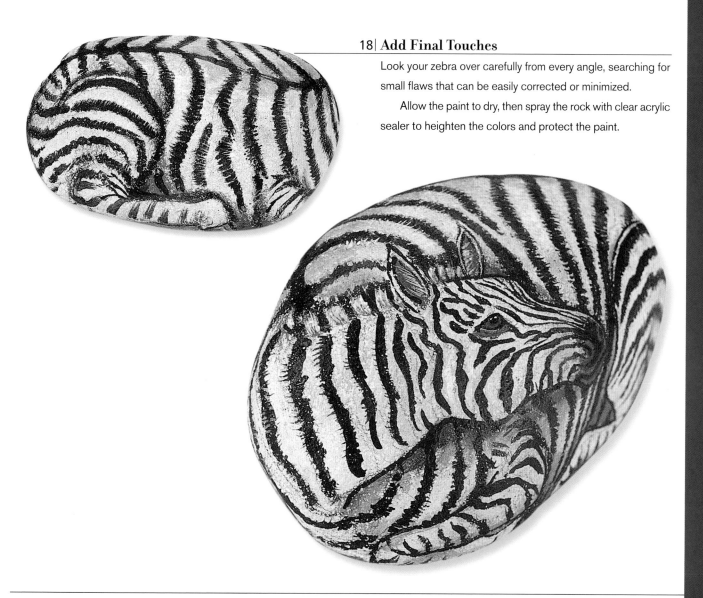

18| Add Final Touches

Look your zebra over carefully from every angle, searching for small flaws that can be easily corrected or minimized.

Allow the paint to dry, then spray the rock with clear acrylic sealer to heighten the colors and protect the paint.

Expand your zebra herd by making standing zebras. To do this, you will want to create an augmented neck to attach to your rock base. You can use pieces of gravel, glued together to build up the neck and head. This will give your zebra rock a graceful form that is strikingly realistic.

I used 521 Clear Glue to join pieces of gravel chosen for their shape and the way their facets fit together. Crumpled aluminum foil supports the gravel additions as they dry. Use a larger, more triangular-shaped piece for the head.

When dry, fill in the joints with wood filler and again cradle with foil, as the wood filler will soften the glue before both cure. The resulting bond will be surprisingly secure. You can also use wood filler to add more realistic contours to the head shape, building up the eye area and shaping the muzzle. I glued on bits of marble chips designed for fish aquariums to serve as ears.

For step-by-step instruction for creating an augmented neck, refer to the giraffe project on pages 94–95, steps 3 and 4.

Elephant Habitat

Despite their massive size, it is easy to see why these gentle giants are a favorite at any zoo. Watch them interact with other elephants, gently stroking one another with their trunks or leaning companionably together under the shade of a tree, and you will begin to appreciate how truly sociable and devoted they are to one another. At the zoo in Cincinnati, I was on hand as the keepers filled a wading pool for a baby elephant who paced impatiently until the gate was opened. It was such a delight to watch that little guy run and literally leap into the pool just as any three-year-old human might have done. The combination of size and intelligence makes elephants one of the most arresting and admirable members of the animal kingdom.

what you'll need

DecoArt Patio Paints in Wrought Iron Black · Cloud White · Pinecone Brown · Sunflower Yellow · large stiff-bristled flat brush · small and medium soft flat brushes · medium shader brushes · no. 0 or no. 1 liner brush · white-leaded pencil · template-making supplies, listed on page 14, optional · clear acrylic spray sealer

1| Choose a Rock

The best rocks for elephants are rounded on top, with flat bottoms that allow them to stand. The sides should curve out, suggesting the bulk of this animal. One very rounded end might be perfect for an elephant in profile while a more blunt or angled end could suggest the turned head I used for this project. Once you've found your rock, scrub it and let it dry. My rock is a little over 5" (13cm) tall, 6" (15cm) long and 3" (8cm) wide. I've painted much larger ones and occasionally smaller ones.

2| Basecoat Your Rock

Mix two parts white with one part black to get a medium shade of gray. Elephants come in colors that range from dark to light gray and sometimes even brown. Add one part Pinecone Brown (which I did for this project) or Sunflower Yellow to warm up the gray paint. Cover the rock quickly, using a large stiff-bristled brush.

3| Sketch the Design

Copy the pattern freehand or make a template as described on page 13. Experiment with placement for the best fit on your rock.

Once the head is in place, the rest of this animal will be dictated by the contours of your individual rock. The front legs are like columns that taper out slightly at both ends. My rock's end is blunt, so I brought the front leg on the far side forward as though lifted in mid-step to fill in that corner of the rock. The other front leg is straight. The back legs are similar in shape, but seem shorter because the tummy line sags lower. Curving the upper portion of the leg line where it extends into the body gives the elephant's midsection a rounded look. Sketch in a second back leg just in front of the first one as though the rock is transparent. On the backside, place the straight front leg as if looking through the rock, then add the two back legs. You can change their position if needed since both sides can never be viewed at the same time.

When painting your elephant, refer to these drawings again for placement of shading.

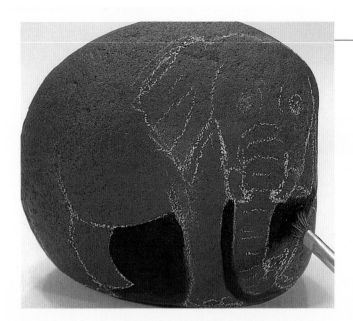

4| Paint Out the Voids

One challenge with animals that aren't curled up or crouching is that there may be large portions of rock that represent empty space. The best way to downplay such open spaces or voids is to fill them with black paint so that they seem to disappear. Use a small or medium-sized flat brush, switching to a liner for tight areas.

5| Paint Over the Guidelines

Use a liner brush and black paint to go over all the guidelines. It is vital that all elements be clearly defined, so paint the outlines bold rather than narrow or sketchy. Outline the eyes and surrounding wrinkles with finer lines. If remnants of your guidelines show, they can be removed later. Darken the opening at the tip of the trunk as well.

6| Create Shadows on Back of Rock

Mix black and Pinecone Brown in equal amounts to get a dark shade that is warmer than plain black. Use a medium-sized shader or flat brush, wiping away excess paint. Scrub on the paint, creating soft shadows where indicated on page 85. Start on the backside to get a feel for how these shadows should look. Shadowing the stomach in a U-shape heightens the illusion of roundness, but leave a narrow line of basecoat along the edge of the tummy to keep it distinct from the dark void below. Shadow the legs, extending some shadows around the legs in partial bands, especially at the midpoint where creases would naturally occur. Darken the very tops of the inside of the back legs on both sides of the rock so that these areas appear to be shadowed by the body. Paint a narrow shadow along the side of the tail just shy of the edge.

7| Continue Shadows on Front

On the front add soft lines in the ears to suggest the look of folds. Shadow around and beneath the ears to help lift them away from the head. Make the head itself more distinct by encircling it with shadows that are widest along the lower half. On the face, use shadows to create sunken eye sockets surrounding the eyes. Move out from these sockets to create a second ring of soft shadows, leaving a lighter rim of basecoat in place to suggest bone structure. Bring a soft line of shadows down the center of the forehead, intersecting it with the outer shadow rims around each eye.

Shadow down the inside edge of the trunk, adding a few dark curving bands to suggest creases. Also shadow along the edge of the trunk tip where it curves up. The tusks extend from structures on either side of the trunk and these, too, should be shadowed as shown to suggest dimension.

Shade the sides of the legs, again including more curved bands for creases. Darken along the bottom of the stomach, leaving a narrow strip of lighter basecoat in place along the edge to define it. Note how the shadow along the curve of the stomach reaches up to blend with the shadows around the head and front leg.

8| Create Heavy Highlights

Mix a small amount of black into white paint to get a shade of gray clearly lighter than the original basecoat. Add a touch of Pinecone Brown to warm the color slightly. Use the same brush used for shadowing, again wiping away excess paint to get a soft, dry-brush effect. Highlight all areas opposite those you just shadowed. Paint them heaviest along the tops of features including the shoulder and along either side of the center spine, the top curve of the head and the tops of the ears. Also apply the highlight to a leg if it's lifted as on my elephant. Lessen the highlights as you work down the elephant.

On the face, play up the ring of basecoat around the eyes by highlighting it, then feather paint out into the cheek areas. Add curves of highlighting to the trunk between the shadowed creases. Give just a touch of highlighting to the tusk socket on the right side. On the ears, place highlights next to shadows to emphasize the look of folds. Highlight along the sides of each front leg as well as along the trunk opposite the shadowed side. Accentuate the shadowy creases along the top of the trunk by adding lighter bands between them. Also highlight along the other side of the tail.

When you highlight the back legs, extend a line of lighter paint along the upper thigh to emphasize the curve of the

stomach. Allow highlights to grow fainter and stop altogether about one-third of the way down. Highlights and shadows work together with the neutral basecoat and the shape of the rock itself to create a magical transformation!

9 | Add Finer Highlights

Switch to a liner brush and add a bit more white to your highlighting shade to brighten it. Loosen the paint slightly by adding small increments of water. Use the tip of the brush to go around the outside edges of the ears, face and sockets of the tusks. Completely outline around the trunk, including the opening at the tip. Go around both sides of all the legs. Reinforce the highlighting along the curve of the stomach. Add narrow horizontal lines of this lighter highlighting down the center of the trunk and at the knees of all four legs. On the near front leg, curve the lines into loose circles at the knee. Move to the eyes and highlight between the darker bags and wrinkles. Add small crescent-shaped lids just above and below the eyes as well as crow's feet to the outer corners to give them more character.

Once these main features have been emphasized, begin adding texture to the skin, creating a random grid of fine lines and wrinkles that crisscross in thin curves as shown on page 85. Making sets of two or three strokes in a variety of directions will help keep them random-looking.

Add a row of short lines along the highlighted edge of the tail, then stroke in a cluster to form a tassel at the tip.

10 | Layer on More Fine Lines

Elephants are known for their baggy, wrinkled skin. Play up this distinctive trait by creating a layer of fine, dark lines. Use black, softened slightly by the addition of half as much Pinecone Brown and again loosen the consistency so paint will flow easily from the tip of your liner brush. Start by adding lines between the fine lines of highlighting down the center of the trunk. Outline around the upper and lower eyelids. Add dark lines between the crow's feet and along the brow ridge, flaring the lines out almost like lashes. Make a set of lines that follow the curve of the forehead and more that arch out from the base of the ears.

11 | Add Lines to Body

On the body, intersperse these dark lines among the lighter ones. Use them to play up the vaguely circular pattern at the knees. On the flank and the tummy, use dark lines to reinforce the lighter crisscrosses below them and also to add texture to areas that have few or no wrinkles.

12| Paint the Eyes

Use Pinecone Brown and your liner brush to fill in the eyes within their dark outlines. There is often a temptation to enlarge the eyes and give them more emphasis, but oversized eyes will give this animal a cartoonish look or make it appear to be a much younger elephant. If needed, use black to smooth out the eye edges or reestablish the outlines.

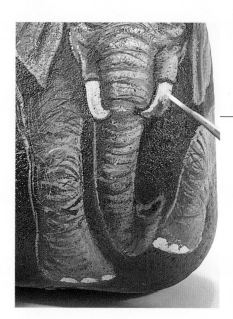

13| Paint the Tusks and Toes

Soften white paint with a touch of Pinecone Brown to make an ivory color. Fill in the tusks and give each foot three neat half-round toes.

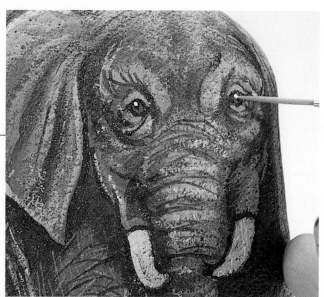

14| Finish the Eyes

Use black and the tip of your liner brush to add a tiny black pupil to the upper center of each eye. When dry, make an even smaller dot of white at the upper edge of the pupil to give the elephant's eyes a lifelike gleam.

15| Add Grass

Minimize the starkness of the empty black spaces around the legs by mixing a touch of Sunflower Yellow into a small amount of white paint to get a pale golden yellow. Use your liner brush to stroke in long blades of grass from the base of the rock upward as shown. Make some of the stems slant sideways as though flattened by those big feet.

An elephant calf could also be placed among the legs to fill up this blank space.

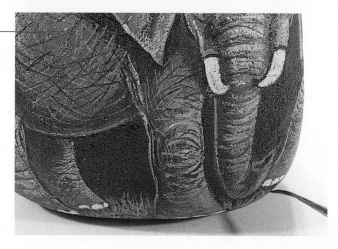

16| Add Finishing Touches

Now look your elephant over from every angle to make sure you have sufficient details. I decided that the dark area below the head on the right side looked unfinished, so I mixed up a little gray paint and added a couple curved strokes in the center to suggest wrinkled skin showing at the chest.

Allow the paint to dry, then spray the rock with a light coat of clear acrylic sealer to heighten your colors and protect the paint. Matte or satin is best on very smooth rocks where gloss sealers may create distracting gleams.

This rock's unusual shape inspired me to try painting from a photo of a baby elephant I came across. I added the ball to fill out the rock shape.

Start collecting elephant photos and you are likely to see many other ways you can fit these majestic animals onto rocks.

More zoo animals to paint

Painting a walrus, with its tusks and wrinkled skin, is very similar to painting the elephant.

Walrus

When painting a walrus, look for a humped rock like those used for elephants. Leave the natural rock unpainted to serve as the base. Mix up a pale gray paint and add Geranium Red to get the pinkish color common to sunbathing walruses. The wrinkled skin texture is identical to the elephant's.

Giraffe Savanna

Would a trip to the zoo be complete without seeing giraffes? Yet fitting a giraffe's elongated neck and stilt-like legs onto a rock is a real challenge. You might get lucky and happen upon an extremely unusual rock shape. If not, there is another solution. It requires a bit of ingenuity and patience, but the reward is a unique and graceful creation that will have admirers asking, "How'd you do that?"

what you'll need

DecoArt Patio Paints in Wrought Iron Black • Daisy Cream • Cloud White • Patio Brick • Pinecone Brown • Sunflower Yellow • multi-purpose cement • wood filler (1.25 oz. tube preferred) • several sheets of aluminum foil • pencil • large stiff-bristled flat brush • small and medium soft flat and round brushes • no. 0 or no. 1 liner brush • template-making supplies, listed on page 14, optional • clear acrylic spray sealer

1| Choose a Rock

Start by selecting a narrow, upright rock with a flat base. A top that is slightly sloped rather than symmetrically rounded is a plus. Make sure the rock is well scrubbed and thoroughly dry. Despite the differences between them, all of these rocks are good candidates to transform into giraffes. The rock I chose is on the left; it's 7" (18cm) tall at the highest end, 4" (10cm) across and 2" (5cm) wide. The top is sloped, which will add to the realistic look.

2| Steady the Base

While good, my rock is not perfect because the base is uneven. I added two small bits of gravel, gluing them in place where the feet would be.

3| Attach Neck Base

Collect an assortment of gravel pieces or small pebbles that can be combined to form a long tapering neck. Like a puzzle, it may take some mixing and matching to find the best combination. Take your base rock along to fit the first piece to the surface it will be glued to. A perfect fit is not required, but construction will be easier if the shapes match up at least somewhat.

Turn the individual pieces around and try fitting together different sides to form a tapering column. Choose a more elongated piece to serve as the head. For my 7" (17cm) tall rock, the neck and head additions totaled 4" (10cm). Once you find a combination that works, keep the pieces in proper order by numbering them and by drawing a line along one side to indicate how they match up.

Use multi-purpose cement to glue the first piece of gravel to the body of the giraffe rock. Press and hold a few minutes until it begins to set, or lay the larger rock on its side and use crumpled aluminum foil to support the gravel until the glue dries. Allow at least five hours for a secure set.

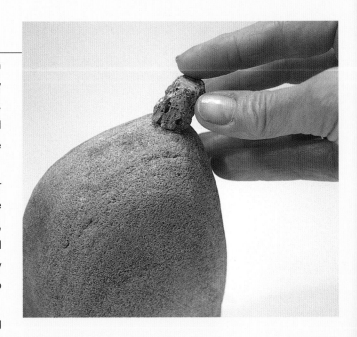

4| Assemble the Neck

Meanwhile, glue the remaining pieces of gravel together to form the neck, cradling them in a piece of crumpled foil. When the glue is thoroughly dry, attach this neck section to the base, laying the rock on its side and using crumpled foil to support both sides as they dry. The edges of gravel may be uneven, but you can cover them with wood filler later to smooth them out.

5| Attach the Head

Stand the rock up and turn it to find the best match of surfaces for bonding the head-shaped gravel piece to the neck. The head can be set on facing straight ahead, tipped up or down or even turned slightly. The surfaces of the two rocks you are joining will likely dictate the direction of the head. If the angle looks unnatural, add a thin sliver or wedge of rock to the neck to change the surface and try again once it dries.

The resulting neck may curve or twist in a way that can be graceful or even whimsical. Due to the nature of the gravel pieces and the way they fit together, your giraffe will have its own unique look. Once it is dry, stand your piece up and check it out from various directions. If you aren't happy with the way the construction turned out, you can snap it apart at any point, exchange one of the pieces or refit a joint. Just make sure you allow the repair to set thoroughly before going on.

6| Fill in the Joints

Because the wood filler will soften the cement, use just enough filler to fill the gaps, lessening the risk of over-softening the glue. Squeeze the wood filler out into the crevices at the joints and smooth it with a wet fingertip to keep it from sticking to your skin.

To ensure that the pieces stay together, use the foil to cradle the neck and head while this first application of wood filler dries, which should not take more than an hour or two.

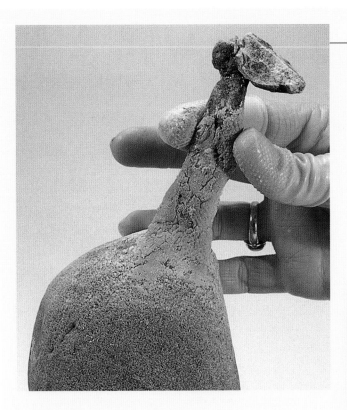

7| Cover Over the Additions

Once the filler is dry, cover the entire construction with sufficient filler to shape the neck into a smooth column. Use the wood filler to modify or enhance the head by adding a muzzle and indented nostrils along with rounded protuberances where the eyes will be. Along the back of the neck you can pinch up a small ridge for the giraffe's short mane. Remember that keeping fingers wet prevents the wood filler from sticking. You may also use rubber gloves or little fingertip protectors. Lay the rock down and cradle the newly covered neck in aluminum foil while it dries. If at any point your construction comes apart, glue it back together and again wait overnight to add filler.

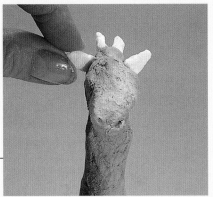

8| Add Ears and Horns

At the top back of the head, build up a heavy ridge and insert two small, cylindrical rock slivers to form horns. Next select a pair of matching flat oval pieces for the ears. White marble chips used to cover the bottoms of fish aquariums make excellent ears and horns. They attach more securely if the ends are flat, and these chips are easily clipped with a pair of sturdy scissors. Use a tiny drop of glue on either side of the top of the head, pressing and holding the ears in place for several minutes until they stay. Once the glue dries, use wood filler to cover the joints at the base. The tip of a paintbrush or a toothpick makes a good tool for smoothing and shaping the filler as it dries.

9| Sketch on the Features

Use a pencil to sketch on the legs and the curved, slanting line of the tummy. Generally the legs will be about the same length as the neck and head, but yours will depend on your rock. It is better to have overly long legs than too bulky a body.

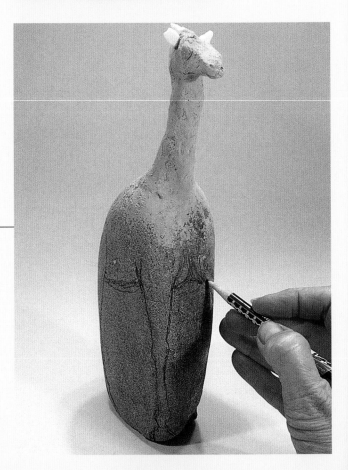

The back legs have distinctive crooks while the front legs have rounded, knobby knees. You can sketch on the legs freehand or create templates from the pattern (as described on page 9) to trace around. Since every rock is a little different, try to fit your legs to the angles of your rock as much as possible. Slant the stomach line down from front to back. At the rear end draw a narrow, tapering tail that hangs nearly to the base of the rock.

When you're placing the spots, refer to these drawings again for guidance.

10 | Paint the Basecoat

Use black paint and a large stiff-bristled flat brush to fill in the spaces around and between all the legs and around the tail in back. Switch to Daisy Cream to fill in the giraffe. You may need a smaller brush to paint the tail.

For subtle contrast, use white paint to lighten the lower third of the body all the way around, as well as along the inside curves of the back legs down to the crooks. Add white to the area along the lower jaw and down the front of the neck halfway down. Extend the white at the chest down along the sides of the legs to the knees.

11 | Add Shadows

Start with a small drop of Daisy Cream and add a touch of black, just enough to get a medium shade of gray. Choose a small, worn brush to pick up this paint, wiping away much of it so that the remainder must be scrubbed on. Apply this gray in a slight curve just above the tummy so that a very narrow line of light paint remains uncovered along the edge. Bring both ends of these shadows up to where the haunch and upper front legs join the body. These U-shaped shadows partially overlap but should not cover all the white basecoating.

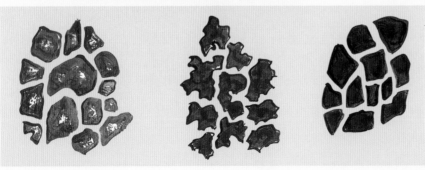

12 | Choose a Markings Pattern

There are several distinctive species of giraffe, each with its own pattern of markings. Some have irregular patches; others have lighter colors in the centers of their markings, while still others have markings with very tidy edges and even spaces. I prefer the look of a more ornate pattern, in the center, but you may choose a plainer one if you wish.

13 | Sketch on the Markings

Use a sharpened pencil to sketch on guidelines, starting with the smaller, more sparse markings around the head. As you work your way down the neck and over the chest and back, increase the size of the patches. Let the pattern evolve so that, while the markings are very diverse, the spaces surrounding them remain the same width, creating a pleasing sense of consistency. As you reach the legs, the patterns should grow smaller and simpler in shape until they stop about halfway down. Don't make markings along the tummy. One exception to the overall randomness of the pattern is the spine, where the markings should form a sort of blocky line of squared-off shapes from the bottom of the neck to the top of the tail. Guidelines for these markings need not be perfect. It is likely you will make changes as you paint them in.

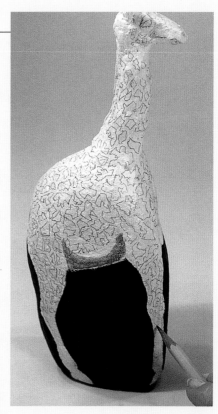

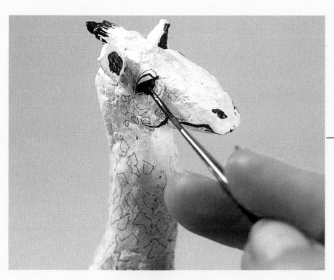

14 | Paint Facial Features

Begin with a small puddle of Patio Brick, adding in enough black to get a very deep brown that is nearly black. Use a damp liner brush to outline and then fill in the centers of both ears, and to darken the tips of the horns. Paint in the nostrils and give the giraffe a mouth line on both sides as shown on the pattern. Use the tip of the brush to carefully paint a heavy-lidded eye on each side just below the ears, and fill in the entire eye circle.

15 | Paint the Mane

Switch to a slightly larger flat brush and use this same dark brown to paint the mane down the center of the backside of the neck. Darken in the flowing fur at the tip of the tail.

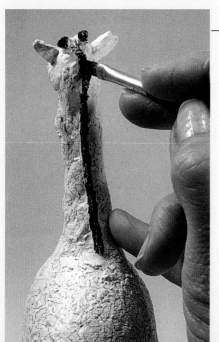

16| Outline the Markings

Add more Patio Brick to your mixture to get a color that is still dark but more reddish brown. Then add a bit of water to help the paint flow smoothly off the tip of your liner brush. Outline the markings, adding more jags if you like.

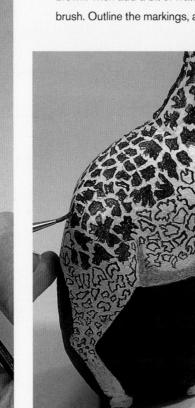

17| Fill in the Markings

Once they are all outlined, lighten the mix with more Patio Brick, and use a small flat or round brush to fill in the markings. Don't go all the way to the edges of the chest or hind end. Before moving to the next step, switch to a liner brush and use straight Patio Brick paint to add a U shape to each eye, leaving a dark center and edges.

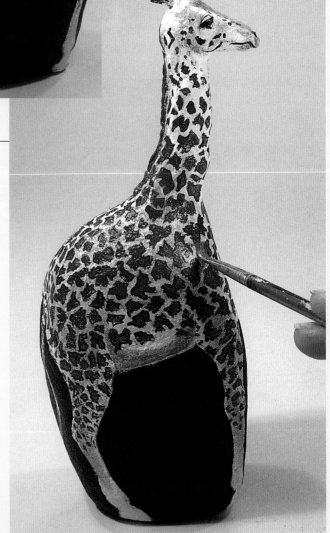

18| Tint the Shoulders and Back

Mix equal parts Pinecone Brown and Patio Brick and add enough water to make the mixture soupy. Use a soft brush to pick up this watery pigment, and wipe off enough to prevent dripping. Apply to the rock with scrubbing motions, starting about two-thirds of the way down the neck and fanning outward down the back and sides. Avoid tinting the tummy area. Extend the tint down the centers of the front and back legs, stopping halfway down the lower portions of the legs. Leave the edges light.

This pale warm tint pulls the marking pattern together and contrasts pleasingly with the areas not tinted. Scrubbing on the wash keeps it soft looking and also helps remove pencil marks that weren't covered up.

19| Tint the Forehead and Face

Use the same color on the head from the base of the horns down to the muzzle, leaving the eyes and the sides of the face plain. Add tint to the area just below the ears on either side of the head, and run a narrow line of tint down the neck on either side of the mane.

20| Paint the Feet

Add a small amount of black to white paint to get a deep gray and use a small brush to fill in the hooves all the way around. The rear hooves are simple curved tops with wider curved bottoms, while the front hooves have a slight dip in the center of the upper line as shown.

21| Add White Detail

With the liner brush, give each eye a tiny dot of white in the center. Add a fringe of tiny white fur lines to the inside edge of each ear.

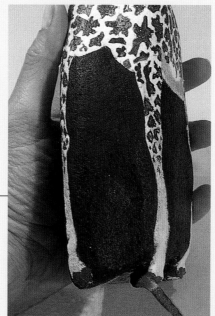

22| Add Dark Detail

Mix a touch of Patio Brick with black and apply with a dry brush to softly darken the center of the forehead, narrowing to two parallel lines down the face, then widening again to darken the center of the muzzle.

23| Paint the Void

Because the legs are so long, the spaces between a giraffe's legs are quite large. You can leave them starkly black, or soften their impact by adding details. To do so, mix equal parts of Sunflower Yellow and Daisy Cream, with just a touch of Patio Brick. Fill in the void from the base of the rock to a horizontal line just below the knees. Turn the rock, extending this horizon to all the sides, but leave dark margins of basecoat in place surrounding the legs and the tail. Add enough water to the mixture to create a filmy wash and use this to fill in and soften the remaining upper portions of the voids, again leaving dark margins around the edges of the legs and below the tummy.

24| Add Grass

Switch to a liner brush and mix Sunflower Yellow and Daisy Cream to stroke in some tall grass stems. Stroke upward from the base to just past the horizon lines on all the sides. Allow the grass to have a random look, with some strokes longer or more angled and others short and straight. Allow the paint to dry, and then spray the rock with clear acrylic sealer to heighten the colors and protect the paint.

25| See How Strong it Is

Like porcelain, dropping the rock or knocking the piece over can damage the neck, but when the additions have been cemented carefully and well covered with wood filler, the resulting piece is both attractive and surprisingly sturdy. I can lift up my augmented rock by the addition and even sling it about without hurting it.

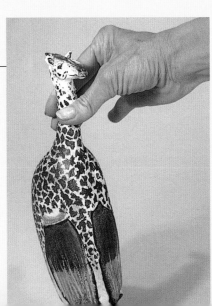

Each of these giraffes sports a different pattern of markings. Variations in both the basic rock shape and the way the addition comes together ensures that every giraffe you create will be unique! If you can't find a suitable rock for a standing giraffe, try making a baby with its legs curled beneath its body like the one shown on page 92.

Use your imagination to think of other ways to use augmentation to enhance your rock animals. Here I've created tusks and a trunk for a truly dimensional elephant!

Welcome to the Petting Zoo

Whether you have a child in tow or are a child-at-heart yourself, the petting zoo portion of any zoo is a special place and not to be missed. Where else can you interact one-on-one with a variety of tame and gentle creatures? Some petting zoos feature mainly young farm animals, now increasingly exotic to our more urbanized population. Other petting areas offer animals ranging from rabbits and mice to guinea pigs and hedgehogs. Here is a chance to feel the texture of a lamb's woolly coat, be tickled by the scratchy toenails of a small rodent or stroke a newly hatched chick. My children recall being surrounded by a flock of inquisitive kid goats that nibbled at their shoelaces and sampled strands of their hair. At another petting zoo we cuddled a litter of young piglets as they tumbled about at our feet. Such hands-on encounters have helped us realize how wonderful and exciting animal life is in all its varied forms.

Chicken
Coop

Newly hatched chicks, fuzzy but still egg-shaped, are a fun and easy subject to paint.

They make an adorable addition to an Easter display, too. Allow the shape of the rock

to guide you in the placement of the chick's head. Look for slight bulges or contours

that suggest where the head might be. This project features a "heads up" pose, but

chicks also look cute with their heads lowered as if pecking at a tasty morsel.

what you'll need

DecoArt Patio Paints in Tiger Lily Orange · Wrought Iron
Black · Patio Brick · Geranium Red · Sunflower Yellow ·
Sunshine Yellow · Cloud White · pencil · paint primer,
optional · medium stiff-bristled brush, optional · small and
medium soft flat and round brushes · no. 0 or no. 1 liner brush ·
template-making supplies, listed on page 14, optional · clear
acrylic spray sealer

1| Select a Rock

Find a small, smooth oval rock, scrub it well and let it dry. The rock doesn't have to be perfectly oval. Mine has one more point-ed end. But it should sit solidly. A line of wood filler at the base can help stabilize a rock that doesn't have a flat bottom. If the rocks in your area are extremely hard and smooth, a coat of primer, such as Kilz, provides a sturdy foundation and also pro-vides a light base for dark rocks.

2| Paint the Basecoat Color

Paint the rock with Tiger Lily Orange. If your rock is dark, you may need to apply two coats, or start with a coat of Sunshine Yellow then cover it with Tiger Lily Orange to get a bright color. Use a stiff-bristled or scruffy flat brush to cover the entire visible area of the rock.

3| Sketch the Design

The layout for this rock could hardly be easier, but you can create a template from the patterns as described on page 13. Use a sharp pencil to give the chick a large oval head that takes up approximately half of the frontal rock area. The head can be placed high as mine is or lower on the rock's front as if the chick is about to peck at something on the ground. On both sides sketch in smaller and narrower ovals for the wings, bringing them to a point toward the tail while leaving the other end open. Just above the base of the rock sketch in a curving line that defines the bottom of the chick while leaving room below to fit the feet. This line can be higher at the head end then swoop down almost to the base below the tail. The legs angle in from a point below the back tips of the wings. Each narrow leg has one back toe and three curving front toes. Add small, widely spaced eyes and a triangular beak to complete the layout.

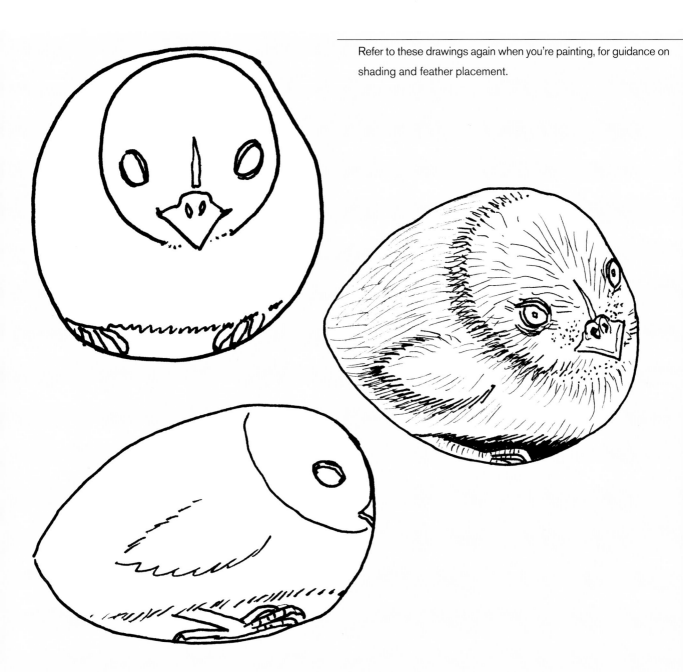

Refer to these drawings again when you're painting, for guidance on shading and feather placement.

4| Paint the Void

Use black paint to fill in the void below the bottom of the chick. Use a small or medium round or flat brush but switch to a liner to paint around the legs and feet.

5| Establish Contours

Mix Patio Brick with just enough black paint to get a deep reddish brown shade. Use a worn flat brush to pick up the paint, wiping away most of it so that the remainder must be scrubbed on. Scrub the paint all around the head, stroking outward. Do the same for the wings along the bottom edge and just barely around the tip. Use this same color and a liner brush to outline the chick's eyes and beak.

6| Fill in the Feet and Beak

Start with a small drop of Sunflower Yellow and add tiny increments of Geranium Red until you get a very soft, warm pink. Use this and a small brush to fill in the beak. Switch to a liner brush to fill in the leg and the long, tapering toes. Though subtle, the legs, feet and beak are a clearly different shade than the body.

7| Layer Feathers on the Head

Start with a small puddle of Sunshine Yellow paint and add just enough water so the paint flows off the tip of your liner brush without being so watery it is runny or transparent. Begin with the outside edges of the head, stroking outward from within the oval to create a clearly defined border of very short, dense splinter lines. Move inward half a stroke and create a second layer that partially overlaps the first, but is not quite as short or dense. Continue working inward until you near the base of the beak, leaving a bit of the orange basecoat showing there. Also leave edges of orange basecoat uncovered around the outsides of the eyes. A narrow line of orange should remain visible right above the beak as well. Refer to the drawings on page 109 for guidance.

8| Add Feathers to Body

Once the head is done, work on the rest of the chick. Leave a narrow gap between the tips of feather spikes surrounding the head and the ones that will cover the body, allowing the shading to help separate and define the two areas. Paint the strokes slightly denser around elements needing to be defined, like the wings. Always work away from the head, with each stroke directed toward the tail as you add layer upon layer until the entire chick is covered.

9| Detail the Face

Use plain black paint on a liner brush to fill in the small oval eye shapes. Underline the V shape of the beak and give it two small nostrils like teardrops. Mix white and Sunshine Yellow to create a pale yellow. Use it to outline the eyes and to outline the inside edge of the beak and the top curves of the nostrils.

10| Paint Pale Yellow Feathers

Still using very pale yellow and your liner brush, add another layer of short spikes around the head, then work into the center of the head as before with this lighter shade. On the body, concentrate the pale spikes in the center of the breast, the tops of the wings, and less densely along the bottom wing edge. Sprinkle them more randomly down the backside.

11| Detail the Legs and Feet

Still using pale yellow and the tip of a liner brush, add a row of tiny, curving lines to the top edge of each leg and even tinier lines to the tops of the toes. These delicate lines give the legs the look of scaly texture. Add a small crescent-shaped nail at the tip of each toe.

12| Finish the Face

With Patio Brick and the liner, outline the eyes and paint parallel lines above the beak. Use a tiny bit of Patio Brick on the tip of your liner to create small speckles between the beak and the eyes and below the beak, to indicate the stubbly feathers growing there.

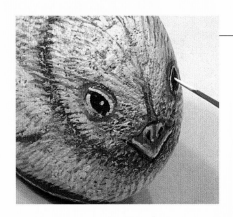

13| Finish the Eyes

Add a speck of white paint in each eye to make it seem like the chick is looking back at you.

14| Brighten the Feathers

Use Sunshine Yellow on your liner brush to add more speckles around the beak and along the lower half of the neck. Sprinkle yellow spikes among the pale ones in the center of the head and throughout the body to rev up the color a bit.

Allow the paint to dry, then spray the rock with clear acrylic sealer to heighten the colors and protect the paint.

smooth the surface by placing a small square of plastic over it and rubbing. Create jagged edges all the way around using the tip of a knife to cut and remove filler in a random way. Paint the eggshell white when it has dried.

For the mother hen, I found a perfect, plump oval rock and added just enough wood filler to build up the comb atop the hen's head. I glued a chunky rock to the back of the rock, covered the joints with wood filler and angled out the sides to form a perky set of tail feathers.

Cover the rock with dark brown made by mixing Patio Brick and black paint. Use black to surround and set off the head and create the curve of the neck, then switch to a smaller brush and use black to layer on V-shaped feathers down the neck and chest and to create a more scalloped looking pattern of feathers along the back and sides.

Mix Sunflower Yellow and white and use this pale gold to highlight and detail the feather pattern and to surround the eye on the head and highlight the edges of the beak. Paint the comb and wattles Geranium Red with a bit of Sunflower Yellow added. Use a liner brush and Patio Brick to add more details and shadings to the feathers.

For the chick in the shell, I used wood filler to create the eggshell hat. Squeeze out a marble-sized dollop of filler on top of the painted chick and allow it to sit for about a minute to lose its initial stickiness. Use a wet finger or damp sponge to flatten the filler over the top of the rock, and then

More zoo animals to paint

Give another feathered friend a try—this little duckling is painted much like the chick.

Duckling

Domestic ducklings are yellow, just like chicks, but wild varieties, such as this baby mallard, have more dramatic markings. Use more white in the layers of downy feathers to make a paler gold color. Then mix black and Patio Brick to make a deep brown for the markings.

Piglet Pen

Like lambs, young pigs are nearly irresistible. Small, sleek and squirming piglets are also inquisitive, bright and fun to watch. Their moist snouts will prod and poke anyone and anything within reach. Hold one too tight and its squeal will signal loudly that it wants to be released. Many people collect pig art and would welcome the addition of a hand-painted rock piglet.

what you'll need

DecoArt Patio Paints in Daisy Cream · Geranium Red · Patio Brick · Wrought Iron Black · Cloud White · Sunflower Yellow · medium or large stiff-bristled flat brush· small flat and small round soft brushes · no. 0 or no. 1 liner · pencil · template-making supplies, listed on page 14, optional · clear acrylic spray sealer

1 | Select a Rock

The main consideration when selecting a piglet rock is roly-poly proportions and enough height to fit the ears either standing up or with folded-over tips. A flat base and plump oval shape make this little rock a good choice.

2 | Paint the Basecoat

A deep, dusky pink basecoat is needed to help set off the lighter fur details. Mix equal parts Geranium Red and Daisy Cream. Use a medium or large stiff-bristled flat brush to cover the entire visible surface of the rock.

3 | Sketch the Design

Once the paint has dried, you can create a template from the pattern provided, as described on page 13, or simply sketch the features with a pencil. Draw the head as a rounded shape, with the snout lines angling out as if to form a triangle. Rather than coming to a point, shorten the snout and give it a semi-circular flat end. Add a rounded angle on the head for the unseen eye and draw the ears. Draw the haunches slightly smaller than the head, and tuck the legs and hooves along the bottom edge.

Refer to these drawings again when you're painting for guidance on placement of shading and on fur direction.

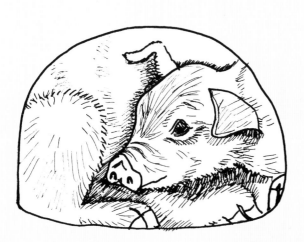

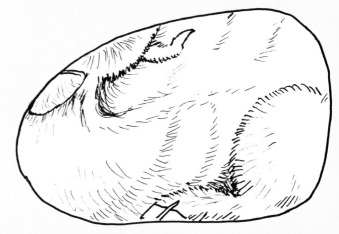

4| Outline the Features

Mix a small amount of Patio Brick into your basecoat color then add increments of black until you have a deep brown color with reddish undertones. Use this color on a damp liner brush to go over all the pencil lines that define your piglet's features. The outlines should not be overly thick, but make them solid rather than sketchy. Don't forget the little curly tail!

5| Add an Undercoat of Dark Fur Lines

Loosen the same paint color slightly with a drop of water and apply fur lines with the tip of your liner brush. Study the lines on page 116 for help with direction. Angle your strokes along the top of the snout, then fan them up and out over the forehead between the eye and the bump where the second eye is unseen. Make a heavier row of strokes above the eye, and another row along the bottom of the eye as shown. Along the bottom of the jaw extend a row of strokes running parallel with the mouth line into the cheek area, and a second cluster of lines that shadows the curve of the head between the back of the jaw and the edge of the lower ear. Add a crescent of dark fur lines to the lower inside curve of the haunches on both sides of the rock.

6| Create Shadowy Contours

Switch to a small flat brush and pick up the same dark color used for outlines and fur, but wipe excess pigment from your brush so that the remaining paint must be scrubbed on vigorously for a soft look without sharp edges. Use this dry-brush method to create deep shadows below the head and at the crook of the back legs on both sides of the rock. Go along the outside edges of the head and haunches with a wide swath of dark shadow. Apply a heavy shadow between the forehead and the crook of the upper ear, and a smaller shadow below the lower ear. Don't shadow the tops of either ear. Along the top of the head extend the shadowing slightly to suggest the curve of the spine. Add two curved bands of shadow to the midsection of the pig on both sides. Also darken the spaces below the legs at the bottom edge of the rock.

7| Layer on Light Pink Fur Lines

Mix up a small batch of the basecoat color using equal parts of Geranium Red and Daisy Cream, then add enough white to get a clearly lighter shade. Use a dampened liner brush to apply this light pink color in a solid mat of overlapping strokes. Check the fur directional guide on page 116 for help in angling these strokes properly as you work away from the nose, down the back and toward the rear end of the rock. On the haunch allow a few strokes to angle upward along the top without obscuring the underlying out-

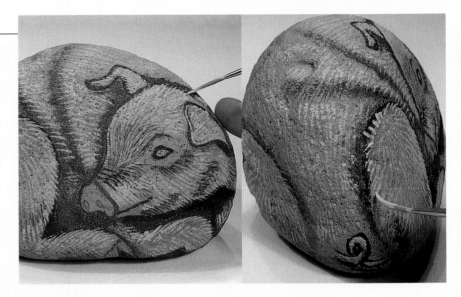

lines. From there move around the curve of the haunch with short, splinter-type strokes. Once you are finished with this step, your entire piglet should be covered with a layer of pink fur excepting the dark shadows where the tips of your fur strokes encroach only slightly. Define the lower ear shape by creating a light outline around its tip right next to the dark outline.

8| Paint Reddish Details

Mix equal parts Sunflower Yellow and Geranium Red to get a warm, reddish orange. Use a liner or other small brush to fill in the cloven hooves on all of the feet. Straddle a few strokes across the bridge of the nose, and surround the eye with this warm color as well. Fill in the flat end of the snout, too. If you opted to give your piglet upright ears, use this color inside them.

9| Add Highlights

Add white to to the mix from step 8 to make a clearly lighter shade and use it to highlight the top edges of the hooves and the top curve of the snout's flat end.

10| Paint Black Details

With black paint on the liner, add two inverted U-shaped nostrils to the snout, then fill in the eye shape with solid black. Also extend the split between each hoof up into the foot.

11| Paint White Details

The addition of a layer of white fur lines will give your piglet its characteristic silvery appearance. White fur also increases the degree of contrast between dark and light areas. Add just enough water to your white paint to loosen it so that it will flow easily off the tip of your liner brush. Go around the edges of your features with a tight row of white splinter strokes, placing them over and around the pink ones you painted earlier. Angle them along the edges of the folded legs and right along the edges of the dark curved lines around the piglet's midsection. When working along the top of the head you may find it helpful to turn the rock upside down. Fan these white fur strokes out over the forehead above the dark lines between the eyes. Add rows of tiny strokes to the chin and along the bottom of the head. Surround the eye with light strokes that remain just outside the darker strokes made there earlier. Add three or four strokes that curve along the top of the bridge of the snout. Don't forget to add white fur layers to the back and ends of the rock.

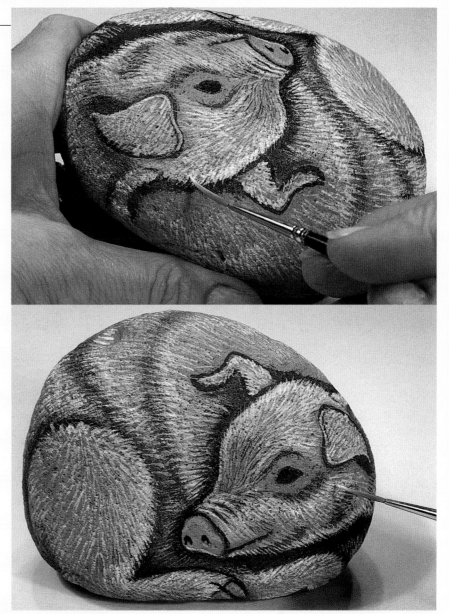

12| Add Golden Details

Before changing colors, add a very narrow half-circle of white to the bottom of the eye, leaving a thin margin of black around the outside edge.

Mix Sunflower Yellow and white paint together to get a pale gold. Sprinkle fur lines of this soft color in amongst the others, mainly down the center of the face, the center of the haunches and lightly through the dark bands of shadowing in the midsection to soften and integrate them. These warm golden fur lines and highlights create a bridge between darker and lighter colors that helps create a soft blending effect. Add pale gold fur lines to the centers of the legs as well, and sprinkle a few in the center of the shadowed area above the crook of the back leg. Do the same in the shadowed area between the two front legs, leaving the outer edges dark. Add an eyelid above the eye and a bit of highlighting below the eye.

13| Paint Reddish Brown Details

Mix Patio Brick with just enough black to darken it to a deep reddish brown and use this to add a small inverted V in the upper half of the flattened snout. Underline around the bottoms of the nostrils, coming up slightly between them to create a short, rounded W. Use this color to add a crease around the upper eyelid and to darken and extend the half-circle of shadowing below the eye. Add a light sprinkling of reddish brown fur to the forehead. Also use it to soften the edges of shadowing around the head and below the tips of the ears. Look for other areas that would benefit from a bit of this detail, but avoid the outside edges of white fur where you want to maintain strong contrast. Don't neglect the backside.

14| Add Finishing Touches

Ordinarily I add a speck of white to my subject's eyes, but piglets have long eyelashes that keep the sparkle from showing. Instead, use pale gold (see step 12) to create a few slanting lash lines along the top of the eye, leaving an edge of the black eye color in place between them. Look your piglet over to make sure all areas are sufficiently detailed.

Allow the paint to dry, then spray the rock with clear acrylic sealer to heighten the colors and protect the paint.

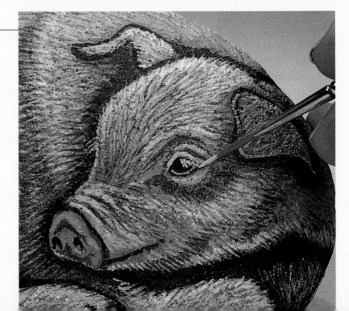

Piglets can be painted in a variety of poses. The rock I painted could also have been done as a head-on view with ears up as the one in the foreground was.

My favorite piglets are the silvery pink ones, but you may prefer to paint speckled or spotted versions. To paint this pig, cover the rock with pink fur. When dry, tint the entire rock with a watery mix of Sunflower Yellow and Patio Brick. Add random black patches, using the tip of a liner to give them fringed edges. Do the same with the white patches.

More zoo animals to paint

Another favorite petting zoo animal is the hedgehog. I made my hedgehog rock "reversible" by painting a different view on each side!

Hedgehog

To paint your hedgehog, mark off the entire white area and paint the remaining area very dark brown using black mixed with a small amount of Patio Brick. Paint the spines with the tip of a liner brush and Patio Brick. When dry, add white tips to all the spines. Paint the white area gray first, and then build up the white fur in layers, allowing some fine fur to overlap into the dark areas. Paint the muzzle with Geranium Red and white plus a touch of black. The paws are pinker, so don't add black to the mix for them, and use more red to outline the fingers. Paint the ears gray with lighter gray edges.

Lamb's Run

From their soft, stuttering baaas to the sweet innocence of their wide-set eyes,

lambs are incredibly appealing animals. It's impossible to imagine not reaching

out to rub that velvet muzzle or pat that fleecy coat. When they are in the mood to

frolic, lambs will kick up their heels and leap about in a way that seems to charac-

terize the term "youthful exuberance." Lamb and lion rocks displayed together

can make a touching vignette.

what you'll need

DecoArt Patio Paints in Wrought Iron Black • Cloud White
• Sunflower Yellow • Patio Brick • Pinecone Brown • Daisy
Cream • Geranium Red • small stiff-bristled flat brush • small
round and stipplers or stenciling brushes • white-leaded pencil •
template-making supplies, listed on page 14, optional • clear
acrylic spray sealer

1| Select a Rock

When selecting a rock, consider the way lambs' ears extend out from either side of the head. Choose a rock with a surface broad enough to accommodate those ears. All three of these rocks have a slight hump that suggests the top of the head, and enough breadth to fit almost horizontal ears. I chose the center rock for this project.

2| Paint the Basecoat

Mix two parts white with two black, and add in one part Sunflower Yellow to warm up the mixture. Basecoat the rock with a stiff-bristled brush. When the paint is dry use a white-leaded pencil or soapstone pen to sketch on the features.

3| Sketch the Design

For lambs, the head and haunch circles are similar in diameter. Draw a smaller circle for the muzzle and place it slightly below the center of the head. Align the eyes and the bottoms of the ears along the top of the muzzle.

Refer to these drawings again when you're painting for guidance on placement of the shading and on fur direction.

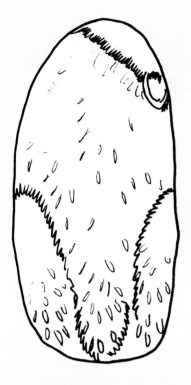

4| Establish Soft Contours

Combine equal parts black paint and Patio Brick to make a deep brown. Apply by pressing or "pouncing" with a short, scruffy brush, one whose bristles are worn and separated. If you don't have such a brush, try using a deerfoot stippler or a small stencil brush. Hold the brush perpendicular to the rock surface and apply the paint with short stabbing motions, turning the brush as you work for a random look. Start on the backside of the rock to get a feel for this technique. Go around the outside edges of your guidelines, giving them bold outlines that are widest in areas that will be shadowed, like the crook of the back leg.

5| Add Contours to Front

Paint contours around all the features on the front side of the rock, adding extra shadows below the ears, along the lower half of the muzzle circle and below the head circle. Darken inside both ears. Shadow more heavily the crook of the leg and the area just above the folded front legs. Contour the forehead lightly with a curved line of shadowing just above and between the eyes. A light scattering of these pressed-on strokes adds texture to the lower half of the haunches and to the lower half of the chest.

6| Add Lighter Color

Building up layers of several colors helps achieve the fluffy look of lamb's wool. Mix together equal parts Pinecone Brown and Daisy Cream. Apply this color most heavily to the tops of elements: the top curve of the head and the haunches, the tops of the rear legs and the tops of the folded front legs. Also use it along the top of the muzzle and the outside edges of the cheek areas as well as on the lamb's back along the top of the rock. Pounce this on as you did with the shadows, pressing the paint on lightly and turning the brush often to get an almost lacy texture.

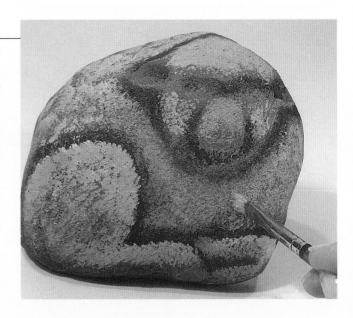

7| Fill in the Ears

To paint the insides of the ears, begin with a drop of Daisy Cream and add in tiny increments of Geranium Red and Sunflower Yellow to get a warm pink. Use a small round brush to cover the insides of both ears. Avoid covering the shadowed base, and leave the dark outlines in place around the edges to define the ears.

8| Paint White Layers on the Back

On the top half of the rock, use your worn brush and pure white paint to give the lamb a diffused layer of white. Begin at the lower reaches with sparse strokes. As you near the top of the rock, gradually apply the white almost solidly.

Switch to a short round brush with soft bristles to add short fat strokes to the haunch. Unlike fur lines, begin these at the outside edges of the haunch by setting the brush tip down solidly then pulling inward to create a teardrop shape. These strokes should be sparse and random in the bottom half, becoming denser as your work up toward the top of the curve. Use the same short, fat strokes to detail the top of the folded-over front leg on that side.

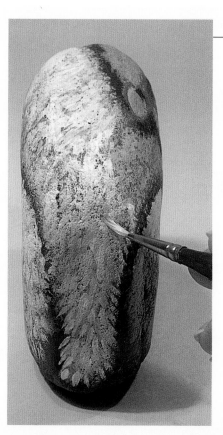

9| Add White to the Tail

Give the tail texture as you did at the haunch, then return to the scruffy brush to fill in the rest of the back. Turn your rock around and detail the fleece on the front haunch and front side in the same way.

10| Paint the Head

Once the body is covered, use the pure white paint on your small round brush to fill in the top of the head with short, thick strokes, leaving just enough space between strokes to give them definition. When the top of the head is covered, outline around the shapes of the eyes with pure white, and go around the outside edges of the ears without covering the dark outlines made earlier.

11| Add More Fleecy Texture

Switch to Daisy Cream to surround the outside of the face with stubby strokes, working inward with subsequent layers until you reach the shadows encircling the muzzle. Use the same color to give more texture to the edges of the front and back legs. Careful layering on of these fat strokes is what gives the lamb its fleecy texture.

12| Fill in the Muzzle Area

Use a small stiff-bristled brush and white paint, wiping away excess pigment so what remains must be scrubbed on. Fill in the muzzle this way, giving the area a soft look while leaving very narrow, dark margins in place for definition. Leave the small V-shaped nose un-covered as well as the lines for the mouth and the vertical connection be-tween mouth and nose. Switch to a liner brush to outline the top of the nose and to fill in the chin with solid white.

13| Fine Tune the Features

Use a liner brush and black paint to go over the mouth line, to underline the nose V and the straight line connecting it to the mouth below. Fill in the eye circles, keeping them small and oval, with short extensions from the outside top edges and down from the inside corners.

14| Detail the Hooves

Still using black paint and your liner brush, outline around the edges of the two back hooves and add a line down the center to create the characteristic split hoof this animal has.

15| Adding More Texture

Now is the time to look over your lamb and determine what areas are in need of more fleecy texture. Scatter fat, very white strokes over the chest, sides and haunch, and any place that seems to need more texture. You can also mix up some medium gray paint and use it sparingly to add fleecy texture in areas where the dark basecoat was covered too completely to provide any contrast. Scattering narrow J-shaped lines about at varying angles makes them appear to be shadowing thick fleecy wool.

16| Finish the Eyes

A tiny dot of white in the center of each eye gives the lamb a life-like gleam.

Allow the paint to dry, then spray the rock with clear acrylic sealer to heighten the colors and protect the paint.

More zoo animals to paint

Make a goat and her kid to join your lamb at the petting zoo!

Mother Goat With Kid

On a rock similar to those used for lambs, you can paint this appealing pair. I used combinations of Patio Brick, Sunflower Yellow and Cloud White to paint and detail the mother. For the kid I chose to use black and shades of gray plus white, while mimicking the mother's markings so that they are similar but different.

Resources

Part of the appeal of rock painting is that the surfaces are easy to find and the materials are simple and few. Most of the materials used are available at any craft or hardware store. However, if you are unable to locate a product, contact the manufacturer below for information on a retailer near you.

Paints
DecoArt Patio Paints
P.O. Box 386
Stanford, KY 40484
www.decoart.com

Brushes
Loew-Cornell
563 Chestnut Ave.
Teaneck, NJ 07666-2490
201-836-7070
www.loew-cornell.com

Wood Filler
Leech's Real Wood Filler
Leech Products
P.O. Box 2147
Hutchinson, KS 67504
620-669-0145 or 800-992-9018
www.leechadhesives.com

Adhesives
Bond Adhesives Company
Newark, NJ 07114
800-879-0527

Painting Pets on Rocks

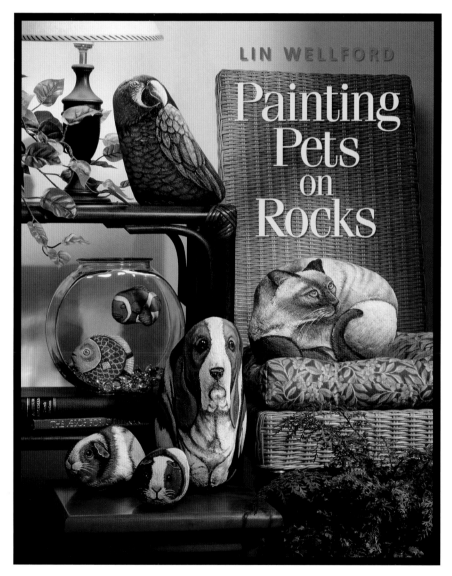

LIN WELLFORD

NORTH LIGHT BOOKS
CINCINNATI, OHIO

Table *of* Contents

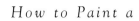

DOGS

136

Introduction

Whether furry, feathered or finned, the animals we choose to live with occupy a special place in our hearts as well as our homes. Capturing the likeness of a beloved pet on a rock is a wonderful way to celebrate that special bond, while creating a lasting remembrance.

Ever since my first book, *The Art of Painting Animals on Rocks*, was published in 1994, letters have arrived from new rock painters all over the world. Many people wrote just to express their excitement at discovering this unique art form. Some wanted me to know they had never painted anything that pleased them before trying rock painting. Others confessed to being so intimidated by art that they hadn't even picked up a paint brush since childhood. But the idea of turning an ordinary rock into a three-dimensional piece of art was simply irresistible, and in the process of painting they uncovered talents they never dreamed they possessed. Even accomplished artists have found that painting on rocks is a way to create wonderful, freestanding pieces that never need matting or framing.

There's no magic to it (although turning rocks into art does seem almost like some mysterious form of alchemy). Painting on a surface that already has shape simply provides a shortcut to achieving realistic results. The fact that rocks are three-dimensional objects means you can paint without worrying about perspective, backgrounds, foregrounds and many other aspects of painting that often confuse and frustrate novice artists. People of all ages have discovered that painting on rocks makes it easier to get realistic results that amaze themselves and others. One painted rock will usually lead to another and another.

An added advantage to rock painting is that it is not possible to ruin a rock. If you aren't happy with your first attempt, simply paint it over and try again. If you decide that the rock you chose was not the right shape after all, it can always go back to being a rock until you think of some other subject for which it may be better suited.

When I was painting my very first rocks, there weren't any other painted rocks I could compare mine to, so I was thrilled with my results, crude as those early efforts were. Your very first rock will not likely be the very best you'll ever do. If it were, there would be little incentive to ever paint a second one. The satisfaction of seeing progress as you gain skills and experience is another rewarding aspect of this unique and exciting art form.

Because of its low-cost, rock painting is perfect for group activities with people of all ages. Scout groups, nursing homes, day camps and school art teachers have all found rock painting to be a great recreational activity. Disabled and handicapped people have also discovered that this can be a satisfying and rewarding—yet affordable—hobby.

So what are you waiting for? Pick up a brush and get rockin'!

Getting Started

The popularity of rock painting is relatively new, but painting on rocks is surely among the oldest of all art forms. In the Stone Age, primitive humans mixed their own pigments and painted the walls of their caves. Now we have modern paints and brushes and countless painting surfaces to choose from. So why paint a rock?

One of the biggest attractions is being able to pick up great art material that's just lying around free for the taking. Even more exciting is the fact that rocks already have their own unique shapes and sizes. What fun it is to find a rock so perfect for painting that it's almost as if Mother Nature herself had sculpted it for that very purpose.

The projects in this book primarily require rounded rocks, the kind found in creek beds, along rivers, or washed up onto beaches and lake shores. Often hunters and fishermen can tell you where to find these kinds of water-tumbled rocks. If you live in an urban area, your best bet may be to locate a landscaping company or a rock yard that supplies rocks and stones for building projects. They are usually willing to sell individual rocks at low cost and will let you select your own.

Small smooth beach stones sold by the bag offer a variety of shapes and sizes perfect for painting tropical fish. Another option is to collect rocks as you travel. Develop the habit of peering over bridges and paying attention

My rock pile—it's doing double duty as a landscaping element!

to rocks wherever you go. Finding good rocks to paint is a big part of what I enjoy about this art form. It's like a treasure hunt.

Look for rocks that are fairly smooth, without jagged angles or broken edges. They can be as small as a pebble or as big as a boulder, but for most people, rocks that are at least as big as an adult's palm and smaller than a basketball are ideal.

Learning to see how various rock shapes can be used is one of those skills that will improve with practice. Don't be afraid to experiment by sketching designs onto various rocks just to see how they might fit. You can always scrub away your pencil lines and try again. For every project in this book, I offer suggestions as to specific rock sizes and shapes to look for, but

keep in mind that there is no right or wrong way to select or paint on rocks. Feel free to play around with the rocks available in your area to see how you might adapt them to various subjects. You will develop your own individual style of painting your own particular rocks. The instructions I give are designed to help you through the learning process, but they are by no means the only way to achieve attractive results.

SELECTING PAINT

One question that often comes up is, "Can I display my painted rocks outside?" Although the quality of acrylic paints has improved steadily over the years, I always recommended against prolonged exposure to the elements, as it may result in fading or general deterioration. Then I found DecoArt's Patio Paint, a paint formulated specifically to resist weathering and designed for porous surfaces like bird baths, stepping stones and ... rocks! I began using DecoArt's Patio Paint for my own pieces and have been happy with the results. However, there are a few colors not yet available, and for those I've specified other brands. If you don't plan to display your rock art outdoors, there is certainly no reason not to use paints you already have on hand. The conversion chart on this page will help you match Patio Paint colors to those of other brands.

I prefer to work with a limited number of colors, combining them to create variations when needed. An easy way to combine paints into the specified ratios is to cluster paint droplets of the same size on your palette before mixing thoroughly.

SEALER

I am frequently asked how to seal the finished rock artwork. Patio Paint has a brush-on clearcoat, or you may prefer to use clear acrylic in spray-on form. Since my rocks are quite rough, I use a spray-on gloss acrylic from the local hardware store. It enriches the paint colors and provides extra protection. If the rocks in your area are smoother, you may prefer a matte or satin finish to avoid a distracting shine. If you don't paint the bottoms of your rocks (and I usually don't, since I prefer to have naked rock showing), seal the entire rock to prevent moisture from entering. I also recommend resealing your creations once a year if they are displayed outdoors.

Patio Paint	Folk Art	Apple Barrel	Delta
Cloud White	Wicker White	White	White
Wrought Iron Black	Wrought Iron	Black	Black
Patio Brick	Huckleberry	Terra Cotta	Dark Goldenrod
Pinecone Brown	Coffee Bean	Golden Brown	Spice Tan
Geranium Red	Lipstick Red	Bright Red	Bright Red
Sunshine Yellow	Lemon Custard	Canary Yellow	Bright Yellow
Sunflower Yellow	Medium Yellow	Medium Yellow	Bright Yellow
Daisy Cream	Tapioca	Antique White	Light Ivory
Antique Mum	Clay Bisque	Satin Cream	Ivory
Summer Sky Blue	Blue Ribbon	Regency Blue	Blue Jay
Sprout Green	Evergreen	Christmas Green	Light Jade Green

BRUSHES AND OTHER SUPPLIES

The rocks in my area of the Ozark Mountains are sandstone and have a texture similar to sandpaper. For this reason, I avoid buying expensive brushes. For delicate fur lines and details, my favorite brush is Loew-Cornell's La Corneille Golden Taklon Script Liner Series 7050 in size 0 or 1. The long bristles will hold a lot of paint and I can use the brush on many rocks before the point begins to wear down. Loew-Cornell also makes some stiff, white-bristle craft brushes that are inexpensive and excellent for rock painting. I use wide, flat ones for basecoating and smaller flats for painting in tighter areas. As they wear down or get ragged, I can use them for scrubbing, a drybrush technique used to achieve a soft, diffused look. I've had some success with Silver Brush's Ruby Satin Grass Comb, particularly on smoother stones. Sometimes the bristles on my older brushes will begin to separate from each other, allowing me to make multiple sets of lines with every stroke, a handy time-saver. Other brushes I sometimes find useful include a small round brush for filling in eyes and noses and a larger, soft-bristle brush for applying watery tints.

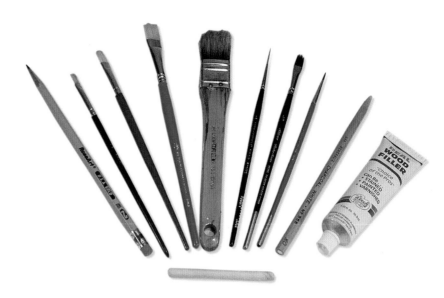

Recommended Supplies

- Loew-Cornell La Corneille Golden Taklon Script Liner Series 7050, size 0 or 1
- Silver Brush Ruby Satin Grass Comb
- assorted inexpensive stiff, white-bristle craft brushes
- white charcoal or chalk pencil
- regular graphite pencil or black charcoal pencil
- wood filler or putty
- spray acrylic sealer in gloss, semi-gloss, satin and/or matte finish

You will also need white charcoal or white chalk pencils and regular graphite pencils or black charcoal pencils, all for sketching designs. I was given a narrow stick of soapstone that has been great for sketching onto dark rocks or over dark basecoats; these are available through suppliers of welding materials.

Occasionally an otherwise lovely rock is flawed by a hole or crack in an obvious spot. Wood filler or putty, available at most hardware stores, is excellent for filling in such spots and can be painted over when dry. Wood filler can also be used to build up a tippy base. I even used it to add ears to a Yorkie pup rock!

BRUSHSTROKES AND TECHNIQUES

Most pieces use the same simple techniques, all of which can be easily mastered. In watching new painters work, I've noticed a tendency to "sketch" with the brush:

attempting to paint lines via a series of small feathery strokes. If you mix enough water into your paint, you should be able to pull a narrow yet bold line in one single smooth stroke, and in doing so have much better control and smoother, more defined lines.

Practice holding your brush almost perpendicular to the surface you're painting on, allowing the paint to flow off the very tip for crisp, delicate fur lines. Try using your pinkie finger to anchor your hand to the rock as you paint for additional stability and control.

An upright brush and an anchoring finger give control.

PAINT CONSISTENCY

Add varying amounts of water to your paint and practice making test strokes on old newspaper until you can make a dozen or more crisp, narrow fur lines with a single brushload. Once you've gotten a feel for the proper consistency, mixing paint will become second nature.

I paint on top of old newspapers, not just to protect my table, but because it allows me to easily wipe excess paint or water off my brushes and to check the consistency of my paint.

Clusters of fur strokes
To create the look of wavy fur, try clustering sets of strokes that fan out slightly, each set remaining distinct from those around it.

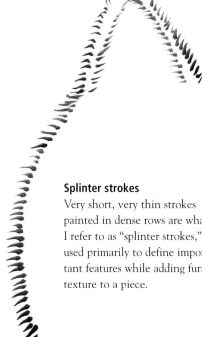

Splinter strokes
Very short, very thin strokes painted in dense rows are what I refer to as "splinter strokes," used primarily to define important features while adding furry texture to a piece.

Layering fur lines
For large areas of fur, create a row of longer strokes, then move halfway up and make another row that overlaps the first. Successive overlapping layers will create the unbroken look of a realistic coat for your animal.

Scrubbed-on paint
Another simple technique, used mainly to create shadows, is to use a stiff or worn-to-a-nub brush with fairly dry paint to "scrub" the pigment into place. Scrubbing with a dry brush yields a soft, diffused look without sharp edges or noticeable brushstrokes.

TINTING

Tinting is another helpful technique for softening or altering fur colors. Like hair dye, tinting is a transparent wash loose enough that lighter lines show through while darker colors are unaffected.

As with most skills, practice makes perfect. Experience will give your work polish and added realism. But even new painters can achieve results they'll be proud to show off. Collect photographs of animals. Often by studying a picture I can begin to isolate geometric shapes that will help me to capture the likeness of a particular animal. See the next chapter on painting your pet's portrait for more information on this. Stretch your skills by tackling new subjects and experimenting with various techniques until you find what works best for you. Experience the magic of transforming a rock into a unique piece of art for yourself. I guarantee that you'll never look at rocks the same way again.

pressing down too hard at beginning of stroke

paint too thick or dry

paint too watery or thin

crisp, distinct fur lines

tinted fur lines

Painting Your Pet's Portrait

Perhaps your pet, like our dog Cookie, is a mixed breed. How do you go about determining what shape rock is best for a one-of-a-kind animal? One way is to take photographs of your pet from lots of different angles. As you can see from my photos, Cookie has many expressions and poses. When choosing one of these photos to adapt to a rock, I spread out the photos, selecting those I thought best captured her personality. I always try to figure out how each pose might translate into common rock shapes. Regardless of which pose you choose, a good selection of photographs will make it easier to paint your rock all the way around. I can use the photo in Fig. 6 as a guide for painting the dog's back, for instance, even if I'm painting the pose from Fig. 3.

Fig. 1
One choice is a sitting up pose. However, Cookie has rather large, upright ears, and fitting them onto a rock would require lowering her head, giving her a "hangdog" appearance.

Fig. 2
In this photo, Cookie's ears were down, making for an easier fit. But this is not her most attractive look.

Fig. 3

Here Cookie is crouching with her head turned. By tucking her feet up against her body and wrapping the tail so it curves around her haunches, I can easily see this pose fitting onto a large loaf-shaped rock.

Fig. 4

This photo gives me a view of the head turned the opposite way in case the rock I select is more suited to placing the head on the right side.

Fig. 5

Cookie's head is not turned as far in this picture as it was in the others. This pose doesn't require so many oblique angles, and it might be easier to execute.

SEEING SHAPES

Learning to spot simple geometric shapes in your subject will be a great help in duplicating your pet's features and making your rock look like its model. In looking at Cookie's picture, it's easy to see the triangular shape of her head and the ovals of her muzzle and haunch. Once you've pinpointed these underlying shapes, they can also guide you in keeping the proportions correct because you can compare their sizes to the rest of the animal and get a feel for how they relate to one another.

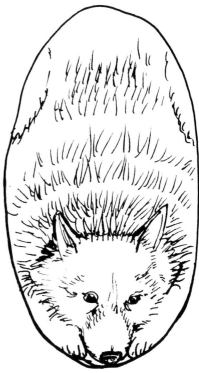

Fig. 6
This photo gave me the idea for yet another pose: Cookie stretched out with her head resting atop her paws. This would work well with a plump, elongated oval rock.

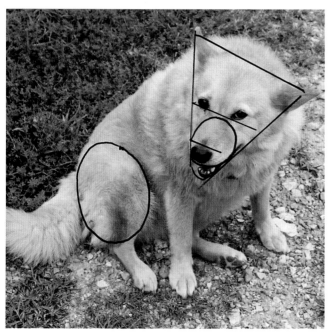

Fig. 7
Superimposing basic geometric shapes onto spare copies of an animal's photo is a great tool for learning how to create your own unique pet portraits. Not only will you be training your eye to recognize those elements as vital building blocks, but they also serve as a guide for achieving proper proportion.

The newest member of our household is Skeeter, a Chihuahua-Pomeranian cross. His portrait could also fit onto a variety of rock shapes. If I were to paint him sitting up, I would darken the area between his front paws, which is the best way to minimize places that you'd like to pretend aren't there. Can you see the geometric shapes in his furry little face?

As with any other endeavor, practice will make a big difference in your results. Give yourself permission to experiment, and keep in mind that it is not possible to ruin a rock! You can resketch and even repaint any rock until you are satisfied with the results.

SELECTING COLORS

When it comes to color, new painters are sometimes uncertain and want to be told what colors should be used where. But if your pet isn't one featured in this book, here's a simple technique for determining what colors you'll need to purchase or mix.

Study one of your photographs to determine which color is the lightest. For dogs that are basically one color, the lightest colors will usually be found along the top of the head, back, and haunches. Cookie's lightest areas (also called highlighted areas) are a very pale cream color that I made by adding a tiny amount of Sunflower Yellow to white paint.

Next, look for the darkest colors. If you find yourself distracted by other details, try cutting a small circle or square from a piece of paper and using it to block out all but the area you want to focus on. Decide what color that area really is. On Cookie, the darkest shadows are a deep brown with a reddish undertone, so I added black to Patio Brick until I reached a color that looked right. Experiment with mixing colors and dabbing them on clear plastic over your photo until you're satisfied that you've gotten a close match.

Usually the basecoat color will fall somewhere between the darkest and lightest colors. In Cookie's case, the basecoat I selected was a reddish-gold color made by combining Patio Brick and Sunflower Yellow.

lightest color for highlighting

mid-value for basecoat

darkest color for shading and details

In this picture, you can see how these three colors work together to establish the shadows, highlights and contrasts needed to create a realistic fur texture.

How to Paint a
Tropical Fish

Tropical fish are treasured for their jewel-like colors and fanciful designs. It's hard to imagine a color combination Mother Nature hasn't tried. Their wide variety of shapes also make fish an exciting subject for rock painting. Paint individual fish on rocks ranging in size from tiny pebbles to whoppers. Look for rocks that are fairly flat and smooth. River rocks are ideal, but you can transform broken bits of fieldstone into attractive fish art, too. Fish rocks can be as plain or as elaborate as you wish, which makes them ideal subjects for beginning painters and youngsters to tackle!

What You'll Need

- DecoArt Dazzling Metallics in Emperor's Gold
- DecoArt Patio Paint in Wrought Iron Black and Cloud White
- Plaid FolkArt acrylic in Teal
- Plaid Apple Barrel acrylic in Wild Iris
- no. 4 or 6 stiff, flat brush
- no. 2 round brush
- Loew-Cornell script liner, no. 1
- white charcoal pencil
- clear acrylic gloss sealer

1 Choose your rock.

See how I used different sizes and shapes of rocks to represent different types of fish. There are so many kinds of fish, you should have no trouble finding a rock that works. Just make sure it's reasonably flat.

2 Lay out your design.

The rock I've chosen is a slightly irregular oval, almost a teardrop shape not much thicker than a fluffy pancake. My rock measures 4" (10cm) long and 3" (7.5cm) wide, about the diameter of an adult's palm. This is an excellent size to begin with as the details will be easy to master.

Use a white charcoal pencil to sketch the fishy features. Since my rock narrows slightly at one end, I'm designating this as the mouth area.

Sketch a circle that begins right at the edge of the rock where the head will be. Leave enough room at the opposite end for a tail fin. The top and bottom fins are formed by the curved wedges remaining above and below the body circle. Keep these fins separate from the tail fin by leaving spaces between them. These spaces, when painted black, will create voids that further define the fin shapes.

Next sketch a half circle to create the head shape. Bisect the end with a slit of a mouth, then add an eye. The size and placement of the eye and mouth can vary from fish to fish.

Finally, add a diamond-shaped side fin just beyond the curve of the head. When you're finished, turn the rock over and sketch a matching design on the other side (or leave it plain).

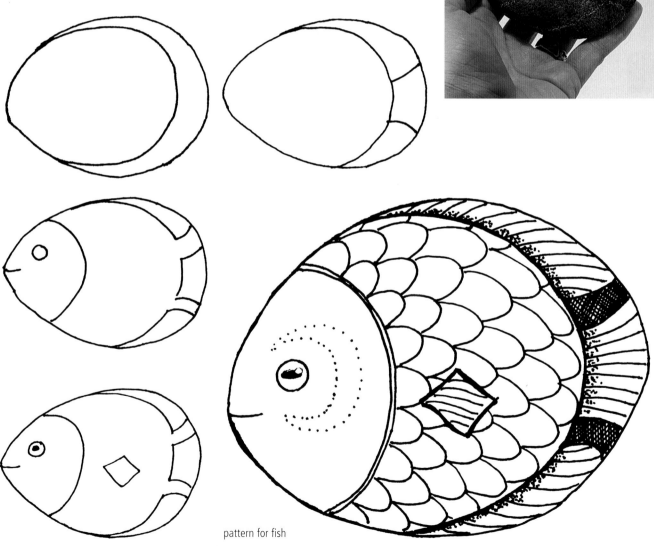

pattern for fish

3 Basecoat the fish.

Use a flat, stiff brush to fill in the body shape with Wild Iris. Make the edges as smoothly rounded as you can. To paint the head and the fins, mix equal parts Teal and white to get a pastel aqua shade. Fill in the head and the fin shapes around the top and the bottom. If you choose to paint only one side of your rock, be sure to wrap the paint around the edges so that no unpainted rock will show. Paint the tail, again wrapping the paint around the end of the rock.

To separate the fins and tail, fill in the spaces above and below the tail with black. Black creates the illusion of empty space.

4 Outline the eye.

Use a script liner and black paint to outline the eye circle. Make the outside of the eye as round as you can. The inside will be covered over.

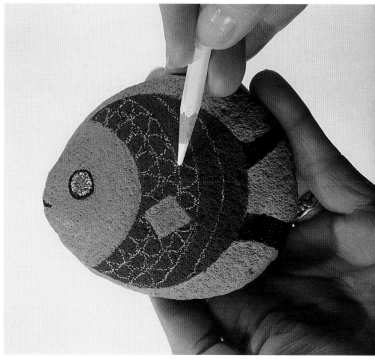

5 Start laying out the scales.

When the paint is dry, use your white charcoal pencil to lightly sketch the guidelines for the scales. Begin by making a parallel curving line just behind the head line. The distance between your lines will dictate the size of your scales. The closer your curving parallel lines, the smaller and more plentiful your scales will have to be. Mine are $1/4$" (6mm) apart. Create a series of these curving lines until you reach the tail end.

6 Finish laying out the scales.

Begin with the space between your first line and the edge of the head. Sketch in sideways U-shaped scales. Fit the next row of scales so that each scale begins at the center of the U in front of it and ends in the center of the next one over. Repeat this pattern until the entire body area is filled in. If you aren't happy with your first attempt, simply remove the lines with a damp cloth and redraw them.

7 Paint the scales.

Use metallic gold and your script liner brush to paint in the scale pattern. Add just enough water to your gold paint to ensure that these delicate strokes will flow evenly without breaking or running. Mixing paint to the right consistency is vital for achieving clean, crisp lines. Hold the brush tip nearly perpendicular to the rock surface to keep the strokes from dragging.

You may find it easier to do a two-step stroke, painting half the scale from one side and bringing the other half in from the opposite side. Practicing on newspaper will help you master this stroke.

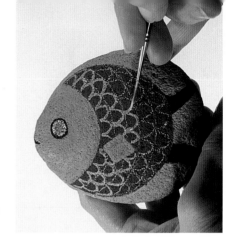

8 Fill in the eye.

While you have gold paint on your brush, fill in the eye circle as well.

9 Define the features.

Switch to black paint, again adding enough water to ensure that your paint flows smoothly. Carefully outline around the body of the fish and around the head circle. Also, outline the side fin.

10 Paint the iris.

Give your fish an oval or round iris in the center of the eye. When the iris is exactly centered, you get a more realistic look.

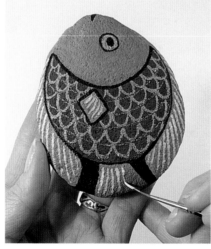

11 Detail the fins.

To detail the fins, create a very pale shade of aqua by mixing a brush tip's worth of Teal into a small puddle of white. Use your script liner to create a series of curving lines angling away from the head toward the tail end along both the top and bottom fins. Fan out narrow lines to detail the tail fin. A set of short, curving lines completes the diamond-shaped side fin.

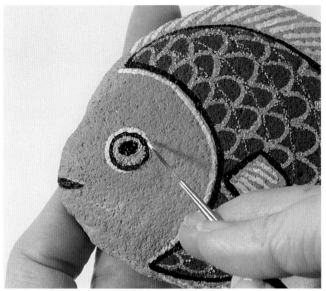

12 Outline the head and eye.
Finally, outline the head shape with this same pale aqua color along the edge of the black outline. Outline around the black eye circle as well.

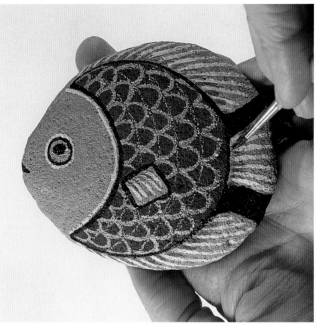

13 Shade the fin.
Switch to a small round brush to darken the spaces between all the fin lines with straight Teal at their bases. Darken the base of the tail in the same way.

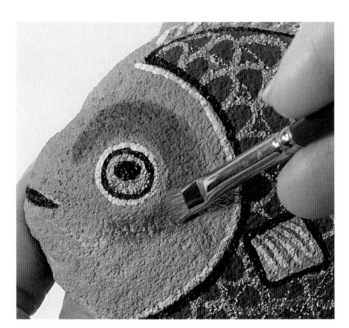

14 Shade around the eye and mouth.
Use your flat brush and more Teal to create a circle of shading that nearly encircles the eye, tapering the stroke at both ends to create a **C** shape that's open facing the mouth. Keep your paint dry for a soft look.

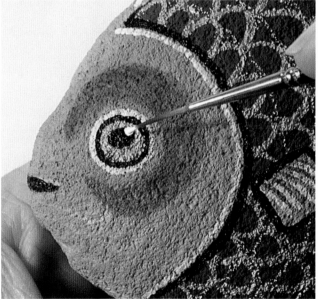

15 Add sparkle to the eye.
Use white paint to dot a sparkle in the fish's eye with the tip of your script liner brush.

16 Finish the fish.

Remove any remaining chalk lines with a damp cloth before you spray or brush your fish with clear acrylic (gloss, not satin) to give the finished piece a shiny wet look. Sign and date the bottom, or, if you painted both sides, sign your artwork along the edge where the upper or lower fins join.

More Ideas

Squared fieldstones, quarried building blocks, even bricks can all be used to create aquariums filled with colorful fish and green water plants. Paint round or oval river rocks to resemble bowls of fish. Try a strikingly beautiful Siamese fighting fish with a flowing scarf of a tail, or a mini school of neon-bright minnows. I've used glitter paint to simulate sparkling scales on some fish. Tulip's Slick Fabric Paint in the little squeeze bottles added eye-popping three-dimensional details to another. A great project for fish lovers is a goldfish pond created on a large, flat stone. Use DecoArt's Patio Paint to create a deep green background, add contrasting fish and some lily pads, then finish with several coats of protective sealer.

You might even want to try creating an impressive sportman's trophy fish (shown on the opposite page). Mount the finished piece onto an oval board for display. (Drill cement screws through the back of both rock and board to secure your trophy fish.)

No need to change the water in this "fish bowl."

You can turn an ordinary brick into a miniature aquarium.

Glue assorted fish to a painted board. A shadowbox frame and glass will add to the illusion.

The tail fins on this "trophy" fish were cut from a plastic milk jug and attached with wood putty.

Here's my solution for a trouble-free gold-fish pond. Incorporate it into your garden landscape by surrounding it with a border of unpainted rocks.

How to Paint a
Guinea Pig

My first pet was a guinea pig, and many afternoons were spent watching my plump, cinnamon-colored friend graze placidly on our front lawn. Rock guinea pigs make great paperweights or desk art (especially for teachers) or lovable rock pets for youngsters not quite ready to care for the real thing.

Guinea pigs are compact creatures without necks or tails, making them excellent subjects for rock painting. Their simple features and symmetry also make them a good choice for beginning painters. The same techniques for creating lifelike guinea pig fur can be used later on more ambitious animal projects.

What You'll Need

- DecoArt Patio Paint in Cloud White, Wrought Iron Black, Patio Brick, Sunshine Yellow and Geranium Red
- white charcoal pencil
- assorted stiff, flat brushes
- no. 2 or 3 round brush
- Loew-Cornell script liner, no. 1
- spray acrylic sealer

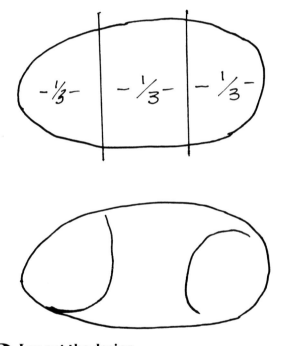

1 Choose your rock.

Begin by looking for rocks shaped like baking potatoes. A slightly tapered or even egg-shaped rock will also work well if it has a flat base. A rock that measures 4" to 8" (10 to 20cm) long is ideal. Working much smaller will result in a pet that risks being mistaken for a hamster or other more diminutive rodent. Examine both ends of your rock and choose the one you think is best suited for the face. If your rock tapers, the slightly smaller end is usually preferred. If both ends are similar, simply use the smoothest and most uniform end.

2 Lay out the design.

Use a white charcoal pencil to lightly sketch the head portion so that it takes up about one-third of the overall length of your rock. If your rock is one of the shorter, rounder ones, the proportions will be more like those of a young piglet whose head takes up not quite half the length. Make the back portion about the same size as the head. The remainder forms the midsection of the animal. Once you've divided the rock as shown, go back and curve the lower portion of the head to create a narrow space beneath the chin where the front feet can be tucked. Round off the tops of the haunches on either side so that they stop about three-fourths of the way up the rock.

3 Draw in the facial features.
Divide the head into quarters vertically and horizontally. Then, divide the two upper sections in half again, creating four pie-shaped wedges. The ears are irregular crescents set at angles so the backs extend slightly beyond the head circle. Rippled edges add realism to the ears. Center them along the lines that divide the top quarters of the head. Keep them fairly small, about as long as the distance between the top points of one wedge.

In the center of the horizontal midline, sketch a shallow, U-shaped nose. Extend a line down from the nose to halfway from the bottom of the rock. Gently curve a mouth line off from either side.

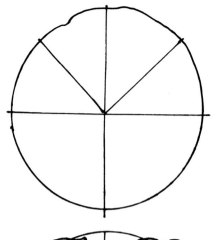

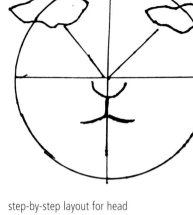

step-by-step layout for head

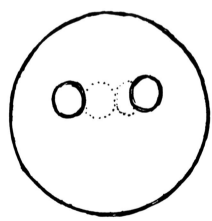

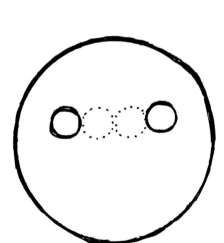

just right

too close together

4 Draw in the feet.
Guinea pigs have well-defined front feet with four small, pointy toes. The back feet are longer than the front ones, and the clustered toes taper to a point. Both sets of feet should be placed along the bottom edges on either side of the rock.

detail of front and back feet

Draw a horizontal line above the midline, not quite halfway to the top of the head. Center the eye circles at the point where this horizontal line bisects the wedge on either side. Both guinea pigs and rabbits have widely spaced eyes. There should be at least two eye widths between them, more if the head end is quite curved. Avoid making the eyes too big. My rock measures 5¹/₂" (14cm) long and the eye circles are barely ¹/₂" (13mm) in diameter. Oversized eyes will give your pet a cartoon like appearance.

5 Sketch in the fur patches.

Nearly all guinea pigs come in white, a golden or reddish-brown, black or some combination of these basic colors. The variety of patch patterns is endless. You can duplicate my choice or create your own. A white blaze up the middle of the face helps define the features. I chose reddish-brown for one side of the face and part of the opposite side of the back. The other side of the face is black, spreading into a larger patch behind the head, then narrowing to a collar to set off the other side of the head.

6 Paint in the basic color blocks.

Use a stiff, flat brush and white paint to fill in the white patches. Rinse your brush thoroughly, then fill in the black patches. Finally, use Patio Brick, toned down with a small amount of black, to complete the basecoat for the fur. Where the different color patches meet, use the tips of your bristles to lightly feather the borders rather than leaving stark edges.

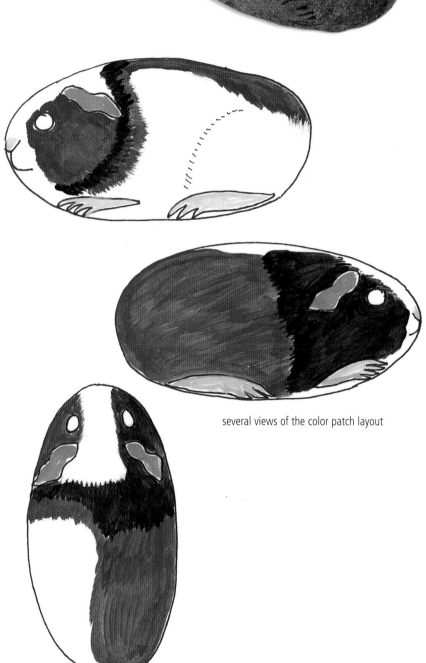

several views of the color patch layout

How to Paint a Guinea Pig

7 Paint in the ears.
To paint in the ears, mix one part Patio Brick with one part white, then add a touch of black to soften the mixture. Switch to a small round brush that allows you to maneuver within the confines of the ears.

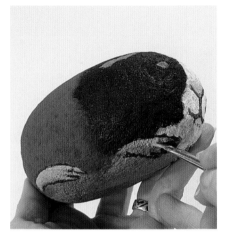

ear color

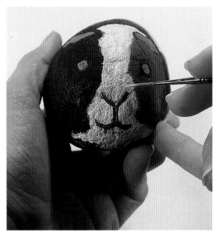

8 Outline the nose and mouth.
Paint over the outlines of the nose and mouth, using the same ear color. A script liner brush will make these lines narrow. Be sure to mix enough water into the paint so it flows smoothly.

9 Paint the nose.
Mix white and Geranium Red to create a medium pink shade. Stroke upward from the tip of the nose using a slightly dry brush to create a soft transition as the pink fades into the white fur above it.

10 Paint the feet.
Use this same shade of pink, slightly thinned, to fill in the front and back feet as well. You may prefer to use a slightly larger brush on the feet for faster application.

11 Blend the edges of the fur patches.
To integrate the color patches in a natural-looking way, begin with white paint and a script liner. Start with the white streak between the eyes and make a series of short, delicate fur lines or "splinter strokes." This creates a fringe that angles out and up from the nose. These strokes should vary in length for a random look. As a general rule, animal fur radiates away from the nose, continuing all the way to the tip of the tail. Fur lines that go every which way will create an unkempt look; layers of uniform strokes create a sleek look. Fur lines will be thickest at their beginnings, tapering to a point as the brush is lifted. It may feel more natural to turn the rock as you paint so you're pulling the brush towards yourself.

How to Paint Realistic Fur

The most important elements for realistic fur are the right brush and proper paint consistency. Mix in enough water so the paint flows almost like ink, without being so watery it will run or turn transparent. Practice adding varying amounts of water and making test strokes on newspaper until the paint is thick enough to be opaque yet thin enough to create slender, tapering fur strokes that don't skip or split. When painting, hold your brush nearly perpendicular to the surface of the rock and apply paint from the very tip.

Do the same splinter-type fur strokes with black paint next, so the edges of black patches blend naturally into the neighboring colors. Repeat with more darkened Patio Brick. When you're finished, the edges of all the patches should be fringed with a row of these delicate fur strokes.

fur direction guide

12 Create layers of fur.

Begin by brightening Patio Brick by adding enough Sunflower Yellow to create a contrasting reddish-gold shade. It's vital you add enough water to the mixture. Thick paint will clog your brush making strokes look smudgy or fuzzy, not crisp and defined. Strokes may angle toward each other and occasionally cross. Make some longer and shorter, but slanting in the same direction.

Start with the brown back patch behind the head, adding a row of long highlighting strokes along the top and down the sides where the brown and black patches meet. Begin your second row so it partially overlaps the first, and repeat these overlapping layers down the length of the back. These strokes will look best if they vary slightly, so resist the urge to line them up perfectly. Leave a margin around the curve of the haunch undetailed for contrast, skipping down to highlight the top half of the haunch itself with rows of fur following the fur direction guide.

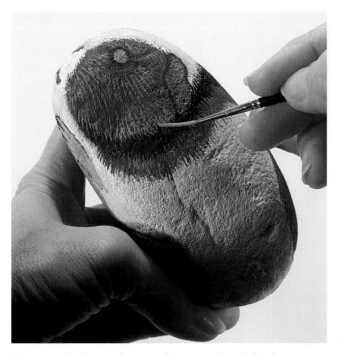

Move to the brown face patch next to detail the features as shown. Be sure to leave a narrow crescent of plain basecoat color below each eye.

To give your brown fur more depth and detail, add enough black to Patio Brick to make a chocolate brown. Use it to emphasize the curved margin between back and haunch, adding several layers of darker fur where the basecoat was left plain. Add another few layers to the lower half of the haunch to suggest shadowing, and to the lower portion of the middle between head and haunch. Also, go over the outlines around all the feet.

Detail the white fur patches using a medium shade of gray made by mixing equal parts of black and white. Gray is used only for shading. Confine your gray fur strokes mainly to the lower portions of the white areas, with a tapered set of dense strokes employed to define the top curve of the haunch.

Use the same shade of gray paint to add furry highlights to the black patch. Leave a dark margin surrounding the eye as before, highlighting just beyond it. Add another curved section of gray fur just beyond the muzzle. Define the head shape with sets of fur lines that begin at the top of the head. Skip over the ear and continue down to end ¹/₂" (13mm) above the front paw. Keep the outer edges of the black patch undetailed. Encircle the eye with a narrow outline of gray.

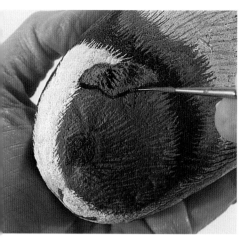

13 Detail the eyes and ears.
Fill in both the eye circles with black paint. Use the tip of your script liner brush and black paint to add a few compact clusters of fur to the ears, then outline around the one on the brown side for added definition.

14 Add the final details.
Switch to white paint and adjust the consistency before making four long whiskers that curve out gently from the muzzle at either side. Soften your white with a touch of black to create a light gray shade, and go around the bottom edges of both ears to set them off. Use the same gray to fan out a set of lines for shading below the chin. Look your animal over to determine if there are any other areas that could use more detailing or defining. The amount and density of the fur strokes is up to you, but the more strokes you make, the more realistic your pet will be.

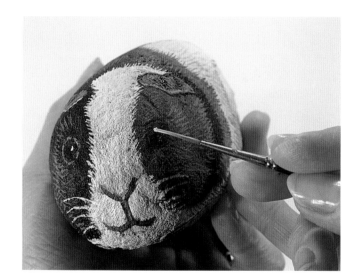

15 Finish the guinea pig.
The last touch is the single dot of white paint near the center of each eye, bringing it to life. When the paint is dry, seal your pet with a coat of clear acrylic. Use matte or satin finish if you are working on smooth, lustrous rocks, gloss if your rocks have texture.

How to Paint a Guinea Pig

How to Paint a Rabbit

Rabbits are similar to guinea pigs and the basic rock shapes are identical. The only differences are that rabbit ears are long ovals placed directly behind the head, and that the feet are blunt oval paws rather than the more rodent-like feet.

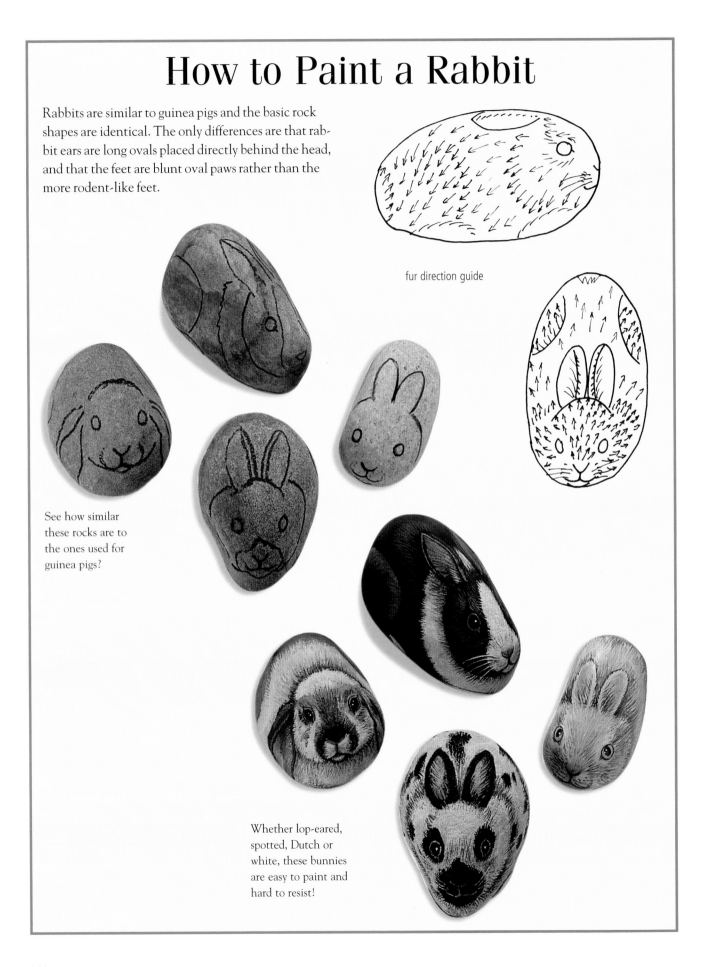

fur direction guide

See how similar these rocks are to the ones used for guinea pigs?

Whether lop-eared, spotted, Dutch or white, these bunnies are easy to paint and hard to resist!

More Ideas

Guinea pigs come in many colors and some varieties have long hair. Domestic rabbits also come in assorted colors and kinds, including lop-eared ones. The hamster is another popular pet that can easily be painted onto a pebble for a "pocket pet."

Wild rabbits are yet another option.

Can't find an oval rock? Try painting twins, or even a whole litter!

Hamster rocks make perfect "pocket pets."

How to Paint a Guinea Pig

How to Paint a
Parrot

With proper care, real parrots (or macaws) can outlive their owners. Perhaps the same will be true of colorful parrot rocks.

A rock parrot isn't likely to whistle or talk back to you, but he won't need to be fed or have his cage cleaned, either. He won't even need a cage! Instead, let him lend an exotic touch to your decor, or perhaps put him to work as a bookend or doorstop. Displaying parrots in your garden is guaranteed to elicit startled double takes.

What You'll Need

- DecoArt Patio Paint in Geranium Red, Wrought Iron Black, Sunshine Yellow, Summer Sky Blue, Cloud White
- regular graphite pencil
- white charcoal pencil or soapstone
- Loew-Cornell script liner, no. 1
- angular or square chisel brush
- small stiff, flat brushes
- spray acrylic sealer

1 Choose your rock.

When looking for possible parrot rocks, select upright rocks that stand on flat bases. They should taper to a rounded top. If the base flares out to one side, that's a big plus. You may even come across a curving rock that will balance on one of its curves to resemble another birdlike pose.

2 Position the features.

Figuring out how to position parrots on different rock shapes may take some practice. The beak is a prominent feature, so line it up along a corner if your rock has one. With rocks that are more uniform, keep in mind that parrots' heads are ovals that are longer from beak to back. The head can be positioned as though the bird is looking straight out, looking back over its shoulder, or turned as though looking away from itself. Use photographs of actual parrots to help choose the most lifelike pose for your rock.

varying rock shapes

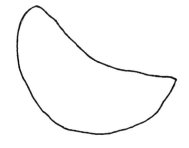

curved rock

I found several potential parrot rocks which stand more or less straight up and one that features a flared base which allows room for tapering tail feathers, making it my choice to demonstrate this project. At the top, my rock has a slightly protruding egg-shaped bulge suggesting the bird could be looking either back over one shoulder or turned sideways to look in the other direction. This second choice allows the frontal display of the colorful wing and tail pattern, making it the more attractive option.

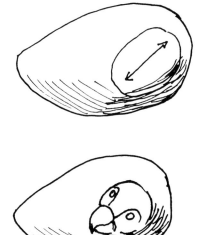

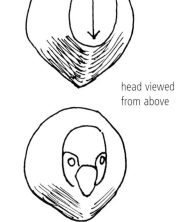

head viewed from above

3 Lay out the head.

The head should take up approximately one-third of the total height of the rock. My rock stands 7" (18cm) tall, so I measured off a head oval that is just under 2" (5cm). Use an ordinary pencil to sketch in the head shape and beak. I've illustrated various head poses. Choose the one best suited to your particular rock. The three-quarter turned head shown at the bottom is probably the easiest and most common.

Copy the appropriate head position onto your rock, being careful to keep the features in proportion relative to the size of the head oval. The beak should take up slightly more than one-third of the total, with the upper curve of the beak extending beyond the head oval. The face patch takes up another third. Since mine is a three-quarter view, a smaller portion of the face patch shows on the other side of the beak; it's a teardrop shape that begins level with the patch on the primary side but remains narrow as it tapers to a point alongside the beak.

possible head layouts

4 Check the features for balance and symmetry.

Draw a straight edge along the top of the beak and set the parrot's eyes into the upper curve of each face patch, resting them on the line formed by the straight edge. This will ensure that the eyes are level and balanced in relation to the beak and to each other. Keep the eyes small to avoid a cartoon look. On my rock the eyes were about the diameter of an ordinary pencil.

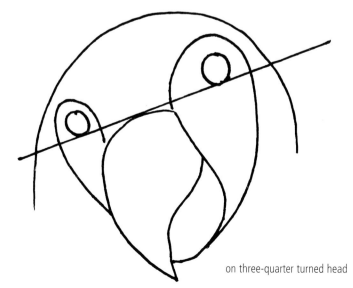

on three-quarter turned head

5 Lay out the body.

Once the head is in place, the remaining features are quite simple. Place the wings just below and to either side of the head, leaving a wide expanse of breast between them. If your rock flares at the base to suggest a tail, the breast should be opposite that tail area. The wing shape is an elongated oval tapering to a slanting point. Square off the tops of the wings. Everything on the backside below the head and between the wings will be the back and tail.

possible body layouts

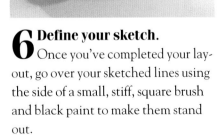

6 Define your sketch.

Once you've completed your layout, go over your sketched lines using the side of a small, stiff, square brush and black paint to make them stand out.

7 Basecoat the parrot.

There are many varieties of parrots and macaws. The one I've chosen is known as the green-wing macaw. Add enough Geranium Red paint to a large puddle of black to get a deep maroon color. Use a large, stiff-bristle brush to fill in every area of your parrot with the exception of the lower two-thirds of each wing, the bottom half of the backside, the beak and the face patches. Don't paint over your black guidelines—leave them for reference and contrast. Paint all the way down to the base of the rock.

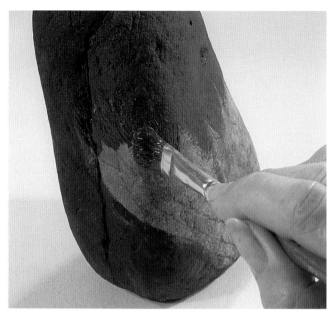

8 Begin painting the feathers.

Rinse out your brush and mix small amounts of black into Summer Sky Blue paint until you have a deep navy blue shade. Use this color to fill in the bottom portion of the wings and backside, using your brush to create a ragged border suggesting feathers.

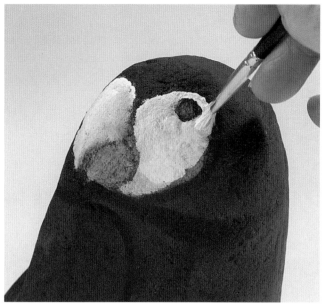

9 Paint the face.

Switch to a smaller brush to fill in the top half of the beak and the face patches with white, leaving the eyes unpainted.

10 Fill in the lower beak.

While the face patches dry, use straight black paint to fill in the lower beak. Also, paint a dark wedge along the bottom of the upper beak corresponding to the lower beak, with the curving top and tip of the beak remaining white. Leave a narrow line of white showing where the two halves of the beak meet to keep each distinct. Check the face patches and add a second coat of white if needed for solid coverage.

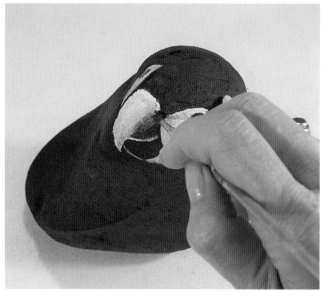

11 Soften the contrast.

Mix a small amount of white into black to get a deep gray and use this color to soften the contrast along the upper beak where the black and white portions meet.

detail of feet

12 **Sketch the feet.**
When the basecoat on the breast is dry, use a sharpened white charcoal pencil or soapstone to sketch two elongated, overlapping feet along the very bottom edge of the rock.

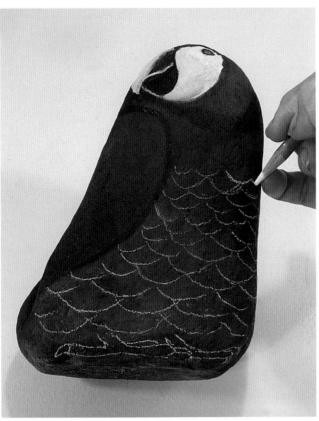

13 **Sketch in feathers.**
Next, create the scalloped look of overlapping feathers on the bird's breast. Begin at the bottom, just above the feet, and make a set of curving lines. Directly above this first set make another row, but start the first curving line so that its midpoint dips down to touch the peak between the scallops below, creating a pattern that continues all the way up to the neck. As you move up, allow the scallops to gradually become smaller and shallower. The scallops do not need to be perfect. Slight irregularities add a more realistic look.

14 **Paint the breast feathers.**
To create a feathered pattern that really stands out, paint an undercoat first. Bright yellow adds warm undertones to the red that follows. Select a brush that will allow you to maneuver in the tight confines of your scalloped pattern. I chose a small square chisel brush that forms a sharp edge when wet. An angular brush will also work well. Use Sunshine Yellow to fill in the scallops, turning your brush as you begin and end each stroke. Note that I did not follow the sketched pattern precisely, merely using it as a guide.

Allow the yellow paint to dry thoroughly. Rinse out your brush and switch to Geranium Red paint to go over the yellow so that no trace remains. Since the undercoat is so dark, don't worry about letting red go beyond the yellow scallops as it will not make much difference. That's why an undercoat is so useful.

15 Paint the red feathers.

Start sketching at the top of the wings and work your way down. The wing feather pattern is similar to the breast feathers, with the topmost row being the same in both size and scalloped shape. But make the subsequent rows of feathers progressively longer as you work your way downward. Allow a few feathers to overlap their neighbors for a slightly ruffled look, and match up the ends of the final red row to the maroon undercoat. The last two rows of feathers in the dark blue area should be almost bladelike in shape, with the tips of the last set reaching nearly to the base of the rock. Repeat this pattern on the other wing. Once again, undercoat the feathers with yellow, but only those in the areas basecoated with maroon. Leave distinct lines of basecoat between each feather. When dry, go over the yellow areas with red as on the breast.

16 Paint the green and blue feathers.

Undercoat with yellow the first row and half of the second row of feathers in the blue basecoated area. For your next step, rather than overpainting with red, mix a small amount of yellow with enough blue to get a medium blue-green and use this to paint over those feathers. For the blue feathers, add just a touch of white to Summer Sky Blue for more vibrancy. Place a bit more white to one side of this blue and mix up a paler shade. When you fill your brush, add just a little of the lightest blue to the edge of your brush so that when you stroke on each feather, the upper edge will be lighter than the center.

17 Define the feathers.

Mix a small amount of blue with just enough black to resemble the original navy blue base color, and use the very edge of your brush to stroke a line down the center of each blue feather for more definition.

18 Sketch the back feathers.
When both wings are done, move on to the back of your bird. Since my rock flares to one side, the back feather pattern will angle in that direction as it travels downward from the neck. If your rock does not flare out, simply allow the back and tail feathers to proceed straight down. Begin by sketching the looping scallop pattern just below where you've indicated the back of the head ends. After a few rows, begin to allow your back feathers to become longer and more pointed, ending them along the edge of the maroon basecoat.

19 Paint the back feathers.
Paint a bright yellow undercoat for the upper back feathers, again leaving distinct borders between each feather shape.

20 Paint the head feathers.
Use the edge of your square brush or switch to a liner brush to create the look of narrow, almost furlike yellow lines covering the maroon portions of the parrot's head, spacing them closely to fill in the entire area but with minimal overlapping of strokes. The direction of these strokes should move out, down and away from the face patches, slanting sideways as they reach the neck to match the scallops below.

When dry, go over the head with red, but leave the dark undercoat showing around the face patches.

21 Complete the tail feathers.

Return to the back of your parrot to complete the tail feathers. Sketch in several progressively longer and wider feather shapes, perhaps including one at a slightly crooked angle relative to the others. The last row of tail feathers should end at the very edge of the rock. Add horizontal feathers along the base of the rock if needed to avoid having any empty spots. Mix up more of the same blue used on the wing tips, again creating a lighter shade that can be used to highlight the edges of the tail feathers. Mix enough navy blue to add spines to the centers of the tail feathers.

22 Detail the red feathers.

Add detail and texture to your parrot's feathers. Begin by mixing black and red to get a maroon similar to that used for the basecoat. Use the tip of your liner brush to create small fan-shaped clusters of shading along the tops of the scalloped feathers. Remember to add water to your paint to ensure that your strokes remain crisp and delicate. Create the same shading lines below and around each layer of feathers on both upper wings and along the back.

23 Detail the green and blue feathers.

To detail the green feathers, mix yellow and blue to get a bright lime green color. Use this as a highlight, giving each green feather a small spine line and a fringe of highlighting texture along the edges. Leave the areas below and around each feather's base undetailed so that they will seem shadowed by comparison. Similarly, mix up a light shade of blue by adding white, and use it to emphasize the spine lines and to add dense feathery details to the upper edges of each blue feather and sparser details to the lower edges. As with the green feathers, leave the deeper blue undisturbed below and around the base of each feather to suggest shadows.

24 Detail the eyes.

To fill in the eyes, use the same lighter green color used to detail the green wings. Make the eyes as neatly round and symmetrical as you can. Center a black pupil in each eye and add a tiny dot of white to the upper edge of the pupil when it is dry.

25 Paint the feet.

Use white paint to fill in the feet. It may take two coats for solid coverage. When dry, use black paint on the tip of your liner brush to add a mosaic of texture to the feet.

detail of feet

26 **Add the final touches.** A pattern of delicate red dots surrounding the eyes is a distinctive trait of the green-wing macaw. Make this pattern by using the tip of your liner brush and red paint to first stipple a straight line that begins along the edge of the upper beak then slants down to the lower edge of the face patch. Make two more such lines of dots above the first, each beginning near the beak and following an almost parallel course to the opposite side. At the eye the dotted lines curve to go around on either side, completing the pattern. On the other side of the face, only those dots encircling the eye will show.

Look your bird over from every angle to ensure you have not neglected any areas. When you are satisfied, apply a light coating of sealer to enrich the colors. If you plan to display your parrot outside, be sure to seal the bottom as well.

Many other kinds of pet birds can be painted on rocks—parakeets and love birds come to mind. By using good photographs, the same techniques for handling parrot feathers can be used to create these and other feathered friends. If you're having a hard time finding a good parrot rock, consider painting a double parrot.

More Exotic Animal Ideas

Parrots and their smaller relatives come in a rainbow of gorgeous colors.

Hedgehogs have become popular pets but a painted one is probably easier to cuddle!

A gray basecoat and flesh colored accents helped bring this rock chimp to life.

Box turtles make great subjects. Choose a rock that's dome shaped on top and flat on the bottom.

Like guinea pigs, chinchillas make cute and compact companions.

Ferrets are easiest to paint in tightly curled poses and will be far less mischievous than their live counterparts.

This albino version of a Burmese Python would charm any snake fancier.

See how this rock accommodates my lizard's long tail while the unpainted portions provide an attractive base? Painting in shadows adds to the illusion of dimension.

How to Paint a
Tabby Cat

Bold black stripes over a creamy background create an attractive contrast that is both dramatic to look at and exciting to paint. This classic tabby coloring is popular, but the same basic instructions for this project can be used to paint a gray or silver tabby with more subtly shaded markings.

To make this project more accessible to people at varying skill levels, it's presented in three phases. The first requires minimal details and should be easy for even beginning painters to accomplish. People with a little more experience may opt to do the additional fur strokes and details offered in phase two. Experienced painters, or those ready to push on to a new level, can add even more layers of delicate detailing. Regardless of your current painting experience, I hope you'll be inspired to achieve a higher degree of realism with this piece.

What You'll Need

- DecoArt Patio Paint in Antique Mum, Wrought Iron Black, Geranium Red, Sprout Green, Sunshine Yellow, Daisy Cream, Cloud White, Patio Brick, Sunflower Yellow
- 1" and ³/₄" stiff, flat brushes
- no. 2 and 4 round brushes
- Loew-Cornell script liner, no. 1
- regular graphite pencil
- spray acrylic sealer

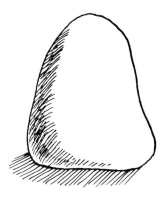
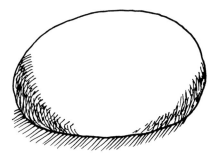

three common rock shapes and three common poses

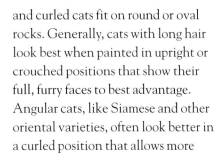

1 Choose a rock.

All the cats in this and subsequent chapters can be done on a variety of rock shapes and sizes. An upright pose works on tall, rounded or tapering rocks resembling tombstones. Crouched positions are more suited to squared, loaf-shaped rocks, and curled cats fit on round or oval rocks. Generally, cats with long hair look best when painted in upright or crouched positions that show their full, furry faces to best advantage. Angular cats, like Siamese and other oriental varieties, often look better in a curled position that allows more room for larger ears. Short-haired cats look great in either curled or crouched poses. It's a little trickier to fit them onto upright rocks, because they lack the fluffy fur coat that helps fill in the wider bottom portions of the rock.

For my cat I've selected an oval rock about 6" (15cm) long, 4" (10cm) wide and 2¹/₂" to 3" (6.5 to 7.5cm) high. Avoid rocks that are less than 2" (5cm) high as your cat will be too flat to look real. Scrub the surface and allow it to dry before applying a basecoat of Antique Mum.

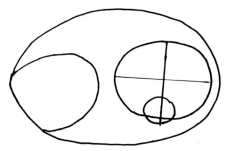

step-by-step layout

2 Sketch the basic layout.

When the basecoat is dry, use a pencil to sketch in your cat's features. If your round or oval rock is fairly uniform, choose the smoothest side for the head. When one end is higher than the other, I select the high side for the head, since it's the dominant feature.

Begin by making a slightly tilted oval head that takes up a little less than half the front or primary surface of the rock. Tuck this oval right against the outside edge of your rock, allowing plenty of room for the haunch and tail. My cat's head measures 3" (7.5cm) across.

At the other end, sketch in an oval for a haunch, similar in size to the head.

The base of the tail begins just beyond the haunch oval at the bottom edge at the back of the rock. My cat's tail measures about 1" (2.5cm) wide and follows the shape of the rock, curving up slightly as it nears the front edge of the haunch, then curving down and tapering to a rounded end as it nears the center point below the head circle. Fit two elongated oval forepaws so that they tuck into the space below the head.

Note that on a more rounded rock there will be less space between the head circle and the curve of the haunch than on an oval rock.

layout on round vs. oval rocks

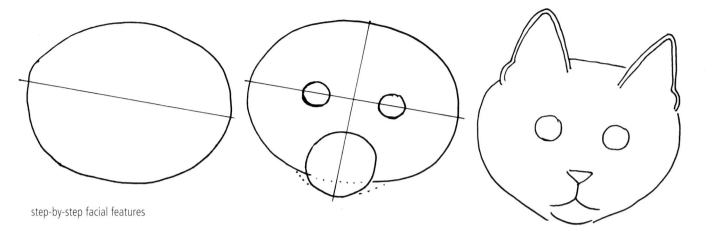

step-by-step facial features

3 Draw in the facial features.
Divide the head oval in half horizontally, angling the line to match the slight tilt of the head. Bisect the oval vertically as well, keeping this line perpendicular to the first so that it's also at a slight angle.

The eyes on my cat measure $1/2"$ (13mm) across. On larger rocks, make the eyes proportionally larger, but keep in mind that overly large eyes will give your cat a cartoonish look. Center each eye over the horizontal line, with at least one full eye width of space between them.

From the eyes, drop down halfway to the bottom of the head, and sketch in a small circle to represent the muzzle. My cat's muzzle is 1" (2.5cm) across, or one-third the width of the head. Allow the bottom portion of this circle to overlap below the head line, forming a small crescent of chin. Fit in a nose triangle so that the top line touches the sides of the muzzle circle near the top, while the bottom of the triangle is even with the vertical line that bisects the head. This will ensure that your nose and eyes are all set at matching angles. Extend a short, straight line from the bottom of the nose triangle, then curve two separate mouth lines off in either direction until they meet the outside edges of the muzzle circle.

The outside edge of each ear should be almost, but not quite, in line with the outermost curve of the head, while the inside line of each ear should line up with the inside edge of the eye below it. On a rock similar in size to mine, the ears should measure $1^{1}/4"$ to $1^{1}/2"$ (3 to 4cm) high.

Before going on, look over your sketched features. Are the eyes the same size and shape? Are the ears symmetrical and properly aligned to the rest of the face? Is the top line of the nose parallel to the line of the eyes? It's a lot easier to make any adjustments now.

4 Create contours.
A $3/4"$ or $1/2"$ (2cm or 13mm) flat brush with stiff bristles is ideal for the next step. Surround the head, haunch, tail and paws with a halo of black paint to make these features stand out. Set your loaded brush along the lines you sketched in, pulling away in short strokes, lifting so that the ends are feathered. Once you've outlined all your main features, fill in the space between the chin and haunch with solid black.

fur direction guide

5 Paint in the body stripes.
Turn your rock around and begin at the top of the cat's head, stroking in a wide stripe that follows the imaginary spine line as it curves down to the base of the tail. Use the same brush and a series of short, connected strokes to create the cat's stripes. Begin just behind the center of the head and curve the first set of stripe strokes so that a narrow space remains between the stripe and the point of the outside ear. This set of stripes should then run parallel to the side of the face to end level with the outside eye. Curve a matching stripe up and around the inside ear and to end up even with the inside eye. Leave a space the same width as your stripe between each successive set of stripes all the way to the base of the tail. On the tail, make as many stripes of the same width as needed to cover the entire length to the tail's tip.

To stripe the haunch (or haunches if your cat is in a more crouched pose), leave an open space along the rounded top of the haunch, then paint in a series of three to four stripes that tilt downward just slightly.

6 Paint the face stripes and define the eyes.
On the face, use the side of your brush to pull narrow stripes from the outside edge of each eye to the side of the face. Paint two straight lines from just above the inside corners of the eyes to the top of the head. Add shorter lines that begin just outside those you just made, angling them away slightly. Rough in a few more lines to fill in the remaining area above the eyes. Below the eyes, paint in dark crescents, leaving narrow spaces between them and the eye shapes. Fan a second curving stripe out from the inside end of the first stripe on each side of the face, and a third one that curves the opposite way to outline the muzzle along either side. Switch to a smaller round brush, one that will allow you to neatly but boldly outline the shape of the eyes. Extend a short line down from the inner corners. Also, outline the nose triangle and the curving shape of the mouth.

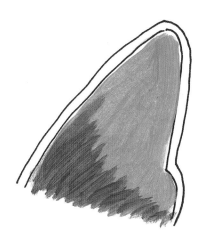

ear color and
shading color

7 Fill in the ears, nose and eyes.

Add a touch of Geranium Red to a small amount of Antique Mum to create a soft pink shade, then add just enough black to tone this pink down. Use a small round or flat brush to fill in the triangular shape of each ear. Create the look of a shadowy base by deepening this dusty pink ear color with a bit more of both black and red. Use feathery strokes and shade only along the bottom of the ears and up the inside angles to suggest depth. The same color can be used to fill in the nose triangle as well.

Mix Sprout Green and Sunshine Yellow to make a vibrant green and fill in the eye circles, leaving neat black outlines surrounding each eye.

8 Detail the eyes.

Next, darken the green mixture by adding black. Paint a C-shaped shadow at the top of both eyes. Clean your brush and mix a much lighter green using mostly yellow. Make a smaller half circle of this highlighting shade along the lower half of each eye. When dry, hang an oval of black from the upper center portion of the eye circle.

9 Add heavy outlines.

Emphasize the eyes by surrounding them with rather heavy outlines of Daisy Cream along both the tops and bottoms, avoiding the dark details. Lighten the top and center of the muzzle along with the chin. Bring out the shapes of the ears by going around them with Antique Mum, but leave a narrow edge of black showing on either side of these lines for contrast.

10 Add muzzle and ear details.

Use a long liner brush or the tip of a stylus to dot curving rows of black follicles across the muzzle. Clean your brush well and add enough water to Cloud White to create a mixture that's loose without being too watery. Test the consistency of your paint on paper first to ensure it flows smoothly without becoming transparent. Pull long graceful strokes from the corner of the base of each ear. Carefully add a set of three to four long, curving whiskers that sprout alongside the follicle dots. Dip the tip of your brush into undiluted white and add one or two white dots to the upper portion of each eye to create a lifelike sparkle. This completes phase one.

Create The Realistic Texture of Fur in Phase Two

11 Add splinter strokes.
Use your long liner brush and loosened Cloud White to begin adding layers of fine fur lines that will give your kitty's coat more texture and contrast. Begin by making what I call "splinter strokes," those short, narrow lines whose bases run together while the tips remain distinct. They help define features the way outlines do, but with a soft, diffused appearance. Make splinter strokes around the top of the haunch and along the top sides of the tail and the paws. Use them to accent the shape of the head all the way around as well. Note that these strokes don't need to be identical in length or thickness, but should be fairly uniform.

To detail the stripes along the cat's body, begin just behind the head and work back towards the tail, using strokes that are longer and more varied than splinter strokes. Allow these strokes to curve and occasionally cross each other in a random and natural-looking way, creating a fringe along the top and bottom edges of the black stripes. Leave the area in the center of the stripes solid black. On the haunch, detail the stripes in the same way.

Shorten the length of your detailing fur strokes back to the size of splinter strokes for the face stripes. Remember that fur always grows out and away from the center of the face, so angle these strokes accordingly as you soften the edges of those markings.

12 Detail the black stripes.

Rinse out your brush and begin adding fringes of black fur to the margins of your dark stripes. Allow these strokes to blend and cross the white strokes as they add yet another layer of texture. The tips of these strokes should encroach into the pale stripes of the coat, but keep them sparse so that the contrast between dark and light stripes is not compromised. Don't neglect the tail as you work all the way back up to the head, where you will also want to scatter dark fur details anywhere the white details need softening or blending.

13 Add dimension to the face.

Make the whiskers stand out by adding a narrow outline of black below each one.

Add a new dimension to the face by using a dry round or flat brush and diluted Patio Brick darkened slightly with black to color in the bridge of the nose, sweeping a little color down either side of the nose as well.

This takes your cat to the intermediate level. Once again you can stop here with an attractive piece you can feel proud of, or you can take it to an even higher level of detail.

Finishing Touches in Phase Three

14 Add gold to the body.

Mix Sunflower Yellow into your white paint to get a pale gold color, then add enough water for proper consistency. Use your long liner brush to begin scattering strokes of this warm gold shade into the pale stripes, allowing them to blend with the white fur and the creamy basecoat.

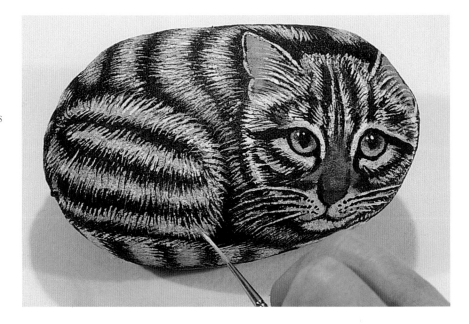

15 Add gold to the face.
Add these delicate gold strokes to the light stripes on the face, too. Sprinkle a fan-shaped cluster along the upper bridge of the nose to help blend the reddish-brown areas into the stripes above.

16 Detail the paws.
How much the front paws show will depend on your particular rock. Mine are mostly hidden but I felt they needed more work, so I added several overlapping layers of golden fur lines to each paw, then used black to add a couple of rather sparse dark stripes.

17 Add the final touches.
Soften your black with enough Patio Brick to create a deep brown, and stroke in a set of very delicate splinter strokes where the mouth lines meet the chin to suggest gentle shadowing there. I also added a few fanned out lines to the center of the nose.

Look your cat over from every angle to ensure that you've added sufficient furry details. A light spray of clear acrylic sealer will add luster and enrich your colors.

How to Paint a
Black Cat

Painting any solid black animal presents a perplexing problem. How do you indicate various contours and shapes without turning black into gray? For this black cat the solution is to create the look of subtle sheens simulating the play of light over the features. Add a pair of startling amber eyes and the effect is riveting.

What You'll Need

- DecoArt Patio Paint in Wrought Iron Black, Cloud White, Summer Sky Blue, Sunflower Yellow, Sunshine Yellow and Geranium Red
- assorted stiff, flat brushes
- old ragged brushes (or a ¼" Silver Brush Ruby Satin Grass Comb)
- no. 4 round or flat brush
- Loew-Cornell script liner, no. 1
- white charcoal pencil
- spray acrylic sealer

1 Choose a rock and basecoat it.

Black cats can be painted in either curled or crouched positions. A crouched pose looks best when displayed up off the floor, while a curled pose is most effective when viewed from above. Look for rocks that have some height to them, similar to a loaf shape. One end may slope down, but at least one end should have enough height to allow room for a head, ears and all. The rock I chose is loaf-shaped, nearly 8" (20cm) long, 3" (7.5cm) wide and 5" (12.5cm) tall. Practice sketches help show how your cat might fit. Scrub your rock and let it dry. Use a large damp brush to completely cover the entire visible portion of the rock with solid Wrought Iron Black. Completely fill in any pits or irregularities as unpainted places will really show up under strong light.

2 Lay out your design.

Look your rock over, selecting the smoothest site for the face. The head should take up a little more than a third but less than half of the total frontal surface visible (for more rounded rocks the front surface will also include the curving top). Use a white charcoal pencil to make a plump oval head that sits far enough down to leave room for the ears. If your rock is quite flat across the top, it's especially important that there be room for the ears. Otherwise, your cat is liable to look earless when viewed from certain angles.

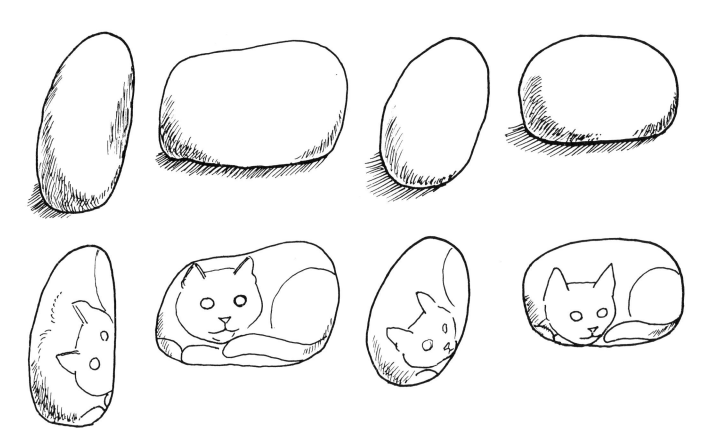

possible layouts for various rock shapes

Bisect the head oval horizontally and center two round eyes on that line. Leave one and a half eye widths between the two eyes. From the inside corner of each eye, run an imaginary line straight up to the top of the oval, and start the inside edge of each ear from that point. Extend the ear lines down into the head oval by ¹/₂" (13mm) or so to keep them from looking precariously perched there. On my cat, the ear triangles measure 1¹/₂" (4cm) from base to tip, and are nearly 1" (2.5cm) wide at the bottom, with the outside edge of the ear attached to the head oval about halfway between the bisecting eye line and the top of the head. Drop down from the eye line to center a small nose triangle so that the bottom is even with the midpoint between the eye line and the bottom of the head oval. From the nose make a short, straight line that drops down, then splits in two, each side curving back to form the muzzle just before reaching the bottom of the head oval.

Sketch a slightly more flattened oval along the opposite end of the rock to indicate the haunch, and bring a thick, sturdy tail up from the base at the end of the rock, curving it slightly before ending it just below and to the side of the head. Indicate a rear foot like an elongated oval beneath the tail. For front paws, add two more ovals, slightly wider than the tail, tucking them in the remaining area beyond the tail tip.

On the backside of the rock, make a matching haunch and rear foot.

step-by-step layout

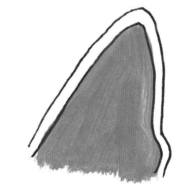

ear color

3 Fill in the ears.
Use a small flat brush with stiff bristles to mix a tiny amount of Geranium Red into a scant puddle of white paint for a medium shade of pink. A trace amount of black will tone this pink down to a dusky shade. Use this color to fill in the ear triangles. Don't paint out to the edges—leave an outline of black around each ear.

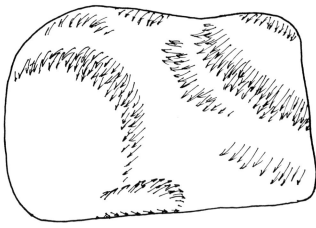

4 Create the illusion of contours.

Select your most ragged stiff, flat brush or a grass comb and mix a very deep shade of gray. Experiment on newspaper to find the mixture of paint and water that gives the look of sets of individual lines with every stroke. Starting with the back side of your cat, create a wide, unbroken swath of these short, highlighting stokes following the curve of the haunch. Consult the fur direction guide to ensure that these strokes angle in the natural way fur would lie. Curving your strokes slightly will give the haunch added dimension.

Leave the lower half of the haunch dark, but add a sheen to the top of the rear foot. Still on the backside, move up to add a set of wide, curving highlights along the top and a curving diagonal swath almost parallel to the haunch, again checking the fur direction guide so that your strokes correspond to the way fur grows in these areas.

Now turn your rock around to the front and define the head by adding a soft sheen at the top and down both sides. Add volume by making a curving series of sheen strokes around the top of the haunch, as well as along the tops of the tail and the front paws. Leave a dark margin all the way around the outside of the head and ears as you lightly stroke in the sheen of shoulders behind them. Note that these strokes should angle upward and outward as indicated in the fur direction guide. At the cat's tail end there may be room between the two haunches for another, more abbreviated, sheen, but remember to leave dark spaces in place between them for contrast.

5 Detail the head.

Add enough white to the gray you've been using to lighten it noticeably. Switch to a script liner brush and add enough water to your paint to achieve a consistency that flows readily from the tip of your brush, yet is not so watery that it runs or becomes transparent as it dries. Begin along the edges of the ears, making delicate splinter strokes so closely spaced that they blend into one another in a continuous prickly line, creating the look of velvety texture while defining the ears. Leave a narrow outline of black showing between the outline and the pink ear color. Along the outside edge of each ear, stop just short of the head and add a small scallop that curves out from the ear line then drops to complete the ear. Outline the nose triangle and cluster a few longer lines above it in an inverted fan shape to indicate the bridge of the nose, ending the lines about level with the line of the eyes. Next, go to the chin area and use a tiny, cupped line to indicate the gleam of a bottom lip just below where the muzzle lines divide. Fill in the chin area with a series of tiny strokes that fan out from just beyond a narrow dark space left to define the lower lip. Layer on more several tight rows of fanned-out strokes until the chin area is clearly defined with fur. Below each eye circle stroke a narrow rim of gray. From the inside corners make a short stroke, almost like a dash, or tiny triangle, pointing down toward the nose.

6 Add more splinter strokes.

Work around the shape of the head with delicate splinter strokes but make them less dense, radiating out like short sunrays. A second, even sparser layer half-overlapping the first (from the inside) should define the head between traces of the underlying highlighting sheen.

7 Define the facial contours.

Use your script liner brush to create subtle highlights, giving the face an indication of underlying bone structure. A row of slanting strokes beneath each eye highlights cheekbones. Give the muzzle contour by highlighting the edges with splinter strokes. Also, highlight the center of the muzzle, leaving dark edges around the nose triangle and between the two halves of the muzzle. Create several layers of highlighted fur in the space directly below the outside ear. Extend the lowest set of these strokes down into the area between the eyes and then back up above the other eye. Leave an undetailed dark place at mid-forehead to provide contrast.

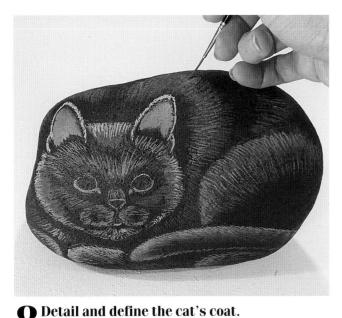

8 Detail and define the cat's coat.

Add texture and emphasis to the sheen areas on the cat's coat by using your script liner brush and the same light gray paint to add fur lines, beginning along the shoulder blades. Create several layers of longer, but still delicate, fur lines along the outer edges of the sheen areas. Bring a delicate set of fur strokes down into the space between head and haunch to keep it from seeming bottomless. Leave the dark margins undefined, skipping over them to work your way toward the tail as you highlight the leading edge of each subsequent sheen area. Along the curve of the haunch concentrate your fur lines to help accentuate this important element.

Add longer highlighting fur lines along the top of the tail if needed to set it off. Then, go back to the base of the tail and create a dense line of shorter, splinter strokes that define the bottom edge of the tail. Use the same technique to detail the front and rear paws, and add a necklace of fur lines in the area showing between the head and the front paws, extending these lines as you curve them around the rock where the cat's chest would be. Don't neglect the backside of your rock, again highlighting the outside edges of your sheen areas, including those along the haunch and rear foot.

It may be difficult to paint these strokes and still achieve a smooth edge along the top of the haunch. If so, simply go back later with black paint and run a line along the outside edge to smooth it down.

9 Tint the gray highlights.

To keep these gray highlights from turning your black cat into a gray one, you can use a simple method that tones them down without losing the texture they provide. Use a large flat brush to mix up a watery tint consisting mainly of Summer Sky Blue with just enough black to create a deep blue-black. Your tint should be so transparent that a test stroke on newsprint allows the letters to show through clearly. It may require some experimentation to find just the right mixture of pigment and water. If your tint is too blue, simply blot it up quickly, add water and a bit more black paint, then try again. Use this blue tint to blend and soften any areas of the coat and face that may have gotten too light, but avoid tinting the fur lines at the outside edges of your features.

adding blue tints

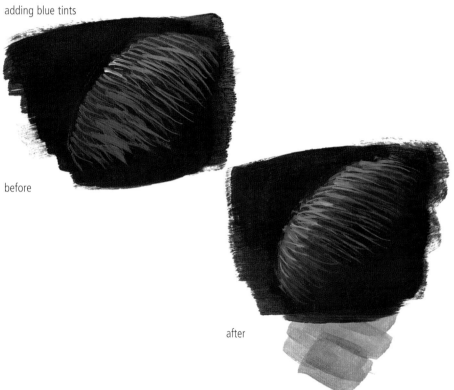

before

after

10 Retouch with black.

Look your cat over for places where your highlighting strokes may have intruded into the dark spaces, lessening the needed contrast. Usually a few dark strokes are enough to correct this. Scatter a few dark fur lines among the lighter ones along the forehead, around the eyes and in the shadows surrounding the head. Add some dark fur lines down the center of the tail and along the paws, so their dark tips blend into the highlighted fur. Try adding some to the centers of each muzzle area, too. You may also need to redefine the tail where it overlaps the front paw to ensure that these two elements are clearly separate.

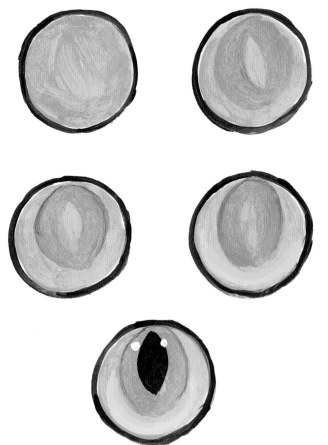

12 Add ear whiskers.

While you have black paint on your brush, add a cluster of dark ear whiskers to the bottom and inside edges of the ears, fanning the whiskers out from the corners.

11 Paint the eyes.

Black cats can have green or orange eyes, but my favorite choice is a bright amber with orange shadows. They practically glow in the dark!

Use a small round brush to fill in both eyes with Sunflower Yellow, leaving a narrow outline of black showing in between the eye color and the gray underlining. It will probably take two coats to get solid coverage. Allow the first to dry before applying the second. Next, add just enough red paint to Sunshine Yellow to make a nice bright shade of orange. Make an inner half circle of orange that just touches the top of the eye, leaving a wider edge of yellow showing in the bottom portion of the eye. With the tip of your script liner brush, add a trace of red to the orange you mixed and use this darker red-orange to outline around the top of the orange half circle. Rinse out your brush and mix a bit of straight Sunshine Yellow with a smaller amount of white to create a bright pale yellow. Use this to create a highlighting ring along the very bottom of each eye, just beyond the orange ring. When the eyes are dry, add a small, oval black pupil to each eye, placed so the top almost brushes the top of the eye, making the cat appear to be looking up.

13 Add the whiskers.

Adjust the consistency of the white paint until it flows smoothly, then apply three or four long narrow whiskers, beginning within the darker area of the muzzle and arching them slightly as you stroke outward beyond the edges of the head. If your whisker lines get too thick, underlining with black will allow you to shave down any excess white.

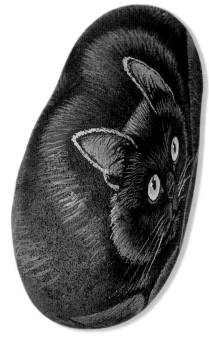

14 Add the finishing touches.

Check to make sure that there is still a very narrow edge of black showing around the bottom of each eye between the gray rims and the actual eye color. It should be smooth and unbroken all the way around, so go over it if needed. Switch to white paint and dab one or two dots on either side of the upper pupil in each eye. Now look your cat over, paying

attention to both ends and back to ensure that you have created enough fur details for a realistic look from every angle. Black cats really benefit from the application of a coat of sealer that will deepen the dark shades further and add gloss to the coat. If you're painting on smooth rocks, use a matte or satin finish rather than gloss to avoid creating glare. Seal the bottom as well if you plan to display your cat outdoors.

How to Paint a Black Cat 199

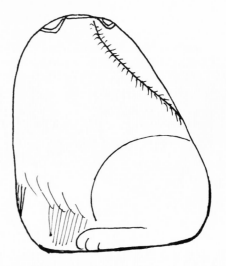

How to Paint a White Cat

Elegant white cats have come to symbolize the most indulged and pampered of pets. Something in their calm gaze seems to assert, "I may be high maintenance, but aren't I worth it?" Long fluffy fur makes this cat a perfect candidate for painting in a sitting pose.

Look for upright rocks that have one flat end to serve as a base and enough height to fit a head at the top, with room for a haunch, feathery chest and two short front legs below. It could almost be a tomb-stone shape, although symmetry is not necessary or even preferred for this project. The rock I chose slopes along one side while the opposite side is more vertical. Overall, my rock measures 5" (12.5cm) high, 3" (7.5cm) thick and is a little over 5" (12.5cm) wide at the broadest point.

1 The features of black animals are defined by subtle sheens while solid white animals depend instead upon the use of delicate shading. Begin by mixing black and white paint to get a medium gray color, then warm it up by adding a brushful of Pinecone Brown. Cover the entire rock with a basecoat of this color. Sketch on your design, and create added dimension by using a darker shade of gray to suggest more depth as shown. Stroke outward from these features to create feathered edges.

2 Next use a stiff or scruffy brush and white paint to highlight those areas that would be the most purely white. Again, pull your strokes outward, allowing the edges to feather.

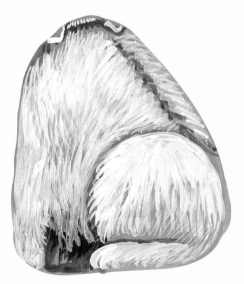

3 Switch to a script-liner to augment the feather edges with additional, longer fur lines, extending them into the solid gray areas to create a blended effect. Leave more gray showing through along the lower portions to suggest shadowing. By alternating sets of gray and white fur lines, you can first define the muzzle area and the shadows around the eyes, then soften and blend them until a balance is reached where the cat's features are discernible, yet the overall effect is so softly understated and the highlights so pure that there is no mistaking it for a gray cat.

4 On the backside use white paint on your stiff brush to create two sets of lines flowing out from either side of a gray spine line.

How to Paint a Black Cat

How to Paint a Siamese Cat

Purebred Siamese cats are lean, graceful creatures with softly shaded coats and distinctive features that put them in a class by themselves. These cats often have long, whip-like tails, angular heads, tilted eyes, large ears and straight, prominent noses. Siamese come in a variety of hues, the names of which refer to their points, meaning the head, feet and tail areas. As with other short-haired cats, Siamese look best in curled or crouched positions. A curled pose is my first choice because it allows plenty of room for those imposing ears. The greatest challenge in painting Siamese cats is duplicating the subtle blending and shading of their coat colors.

What You'll Need

- DecoArt Patio Paint in Antique Mum, Geranium Red, Woodland Brown, Wrought Iron Black, Daisy Cream, Summer Sky Blue, Sunflower Yellow, Cloud White, Light Waterfall Blue (optional)
- assorted large and medium stiff, flat brushes
- no. 2 or 3 small round brush
- Loew-Cornell script liner, no. 1
- graphite pencil
- white charcoal pencil (optional)
- spray acrylic sealer

1 Choose a rock.

For Siamese cats, choose a round or oval rock that is on the thin side, perhaps with some rounded angles suggestive of the sleek athletic build of a healthy, active feline. You can work as large or as small as you wish, but for this demonstration I chose an oval that measures 5" (12.5cm) long, 4" (10cm) across and is just a little more than 2" (5cm) high. Scrub the rock and let it dry. If you are uncertain about where to place the head, try using a white charcoal pencil to experiment with possible combinations. Knowing that you'll be painting over your sketch may help you loosen up as you decide how best to use your rock's unique contours.

2 Paint the basecoat.

Use Antique Mum and a large flat brush to cover the entire upper surface of the rock, leaving only the very bottom unpainted. (For a blue- or lilac-point Siamese, try mixing Cloud White with enough Light Waterfall Blue to get a very pale blue-gray shade for the base.) Allow the basecoat to dry.

3 Sketch the layout.

Envision a broad triangle and you have the basic wedge shape of a Siamese cat's head. For my cat the sides of the head each measure 3" (7.5 cm). Set the head low enough to leave ample room above for the ears. Begin the bases of the ears below the top line of the head so that they appear to be integral rather than perching on top. My ears are 1 1/4" (3cm) high measured from the middle, and nearly that wide at the base. Rest the eyes atop a horizontal line midway down the triangle. On my cat the eyes are 1/2" (13mm) long. Leave slightly more than one eye width between the eyes. Pull a horizontal line out from the top outer edge of each eye, and extend a slanting line from the inner corners to give the eyes their almond cast. The bridge of the nose begins with a narrow pair of lines at eye level. Slightly flare the lines out as they go down, creating a nose about as long as the space between the eyes. Set a small triangular nose leather at the end. There should be just enough room at the bottom angle of the head to fit two curving mouth lines that define the muzzle. Remove the point at the bottom of the head triangle, turning the end into a half round chin. Add curves to soften the sides of the face on either side.

Sketch an oval haunch into the space next to the head. The more elongated the rock, the larger the space will be between head and haunch. A thin, ropey tail is characteristic of many pedigreed Siamese. Bring it in from near the base below the edge of the haunch, curving it gently as you angle it up toward the side of the face, then hooking the tip back in a **J** shape. Tuck two long oval paws beneath the head.

Before going on, place a pencil even with the eyes and another level with the top of the nose. The pencils should be parallel to prevent an off kilter or skewed look. If not, it's easiest to simply change the angle of the nose.

step-by-step layout

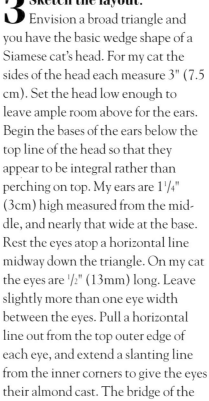

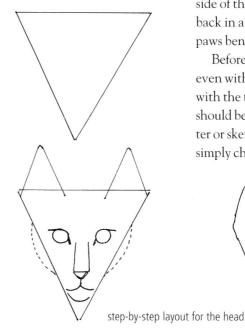

step-by-step layout for the head

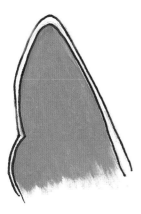

4 Paint the insides of the ears.

Mix a small amount of Geranium Red into a larger puddle of Antique Mum to create a soft pink. Darken this pink shade by adding small increments of Woodland Brown until the color resembles a ruddy flesh tone. Use a round or flat brush to fill in the entire triangle shape of the ears, allowing your brushstrokes along the bottom to be slightly ragged.

5 Paint the points.

Use Woodland Brown and a stiff, flat brush to create a solid mask around the eyes. Darken the muzzle areas and the chin, joining them to the brown mask above. Extend a short, thick line from the top of the eye mask to touch the inside corners of both ears. Paint both front paws and the tail dark brown.

6 Create contours.

Pick up more brown paint, using the same stiff, flat brush. Remove any excess by wiping on newsprint to keep the paint on the dry side. Scrub this paint out from around the head and haunch so that those features are surrounded by a slightly diffused dark halo. Darken the area between the bottom of the head and the curve of the tail, leaving only the narrow wedge between tail and rear foot unshaded.

Turn your rock around and scrub in a curving spine line beginning behind the head and following the natural contour of the rock to the base of the tail. Add two wide, rounded U shapes to represent the shoulders of the cat, and if there's room, skip a space then add a second shaded line, less curved this time, closer to the tail.

How to Paint a Siamese Cat

Finally, remove even more paint from your brush by wiping it vigorously on newspaper before you scrub soft, diffused brown along the top half of the haunch. Make the strokes at the bottom uneven, blending them into the lighter basecoat.

7 Define the face.
Switch to a long script liner and black paint. Add enough water to ensure the paint flows easily without becoming transparent or runny. Outline the eyes, emphasizing those accenting lines extending from the corners. Go around the top angles of the ears to accent them, adding an extra scallop to the outside edges near the base. Define the long bridge of the nose, then fill in the nose leather at the end. Outline the mouth lines.

8 Emphasize with fur lines.
Rather than using solid outlines, define the paws and tail with the texture of fur. Paint in dense sets of short, splinter type strokes that follow the natural direction of the fur (refer to the fur direction guide).

fur direction guide

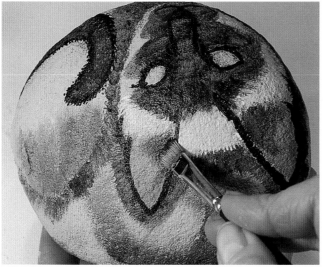

9 Shade inside the ears.

To give the ears depth, use a stiff brush and a combination of brown darkened with black, blotted almost dry. Smudge this color along the base of the ears, fanning up and out from the inside corners. Since these are shadows, they should look soft and blend gradually into the rest of the ear.

10 Create fur texture on the head.

Daisy Cream is a warm, off-white shade that offers a subtle yet effective contrast to the Antique Mum basecoat. Adjust the texture of the paint by adding water and mixing thoroughly until the consistency is loose without being runny. Use the tip of your script liner brush to apply fur lines that are narrow, but not quite as short or dense as splinter strokes. Apply them in overlapping layers like thatch, working your way from the outside edges inward to cover the face around the mask. Again, you may find it helpful to turn the cat around so that you can stroke toward rather than away from yourself. Consult the fur direction guide to help simulate realistic fur growth patterns. Allow some fur lines to touch or cross, but leave spaces between the strokes so that the basecoat shows through. When you reach the face mask, the tips of the fur should slightly overlap the edges of those dark areas.

11 Create fur texture on the body.

On the haunch, begin by outlining the outside curve with the same strokes used around the head, making them a bit longer. Move to the bottom of the haunch and stroke layer upon overlapping layer of cream-colored fur lines. Pull these strokes out toward the edge of the haunch so the fur tapers at the tips. As you reach the upper, darkened portion of the haunch, your fur strokes should create a seamless blending of lighter and darker areas. Allow fur lines to become gradually sparser until, at the top, you sprinkle in a few for continuity, leaving most of the dark undercoat exposed.

too much initial pressure can create knobs on your fur strokes

12 Detail the back.

This fur will be much easier to paint if the rock is turned around. Begin your first fur lines just inside the dark shadows surrounding the head. Use the fur direction guide to aid in determining how to angle the strokes as you apply layer upon layer until the tips of your strokes reach into the next area of contouring brown at the shoulders. Skip down to the next area of basecoat and repeat the process until the entire back portion of the cat has been detailed.

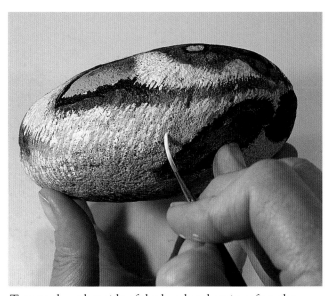

Turn to the other side of the head and again soften the dark shadows by adding a fringe of pale strokes along the edge. Continue to add more fur layers until you reach the bottom edge of the rock.

13 Detail the remaining areas.

Move to the area between the curving tail and lower portion of the face. Leave a margin of brown contouring shadows untouched, using narrow overlapping fur lines to soften the contrast between dark and light areas. These strokes should follow the curving shape of the rock, becoming more sparse near the area between paw and tail.

14 Add more definition to the face.

Add enough black to Woodland Brown to get a deeper dark brown. With a script liner brush, add several delicate layers of fur lines around the inside edges of the mask and muzzle, with just the tips extending beyond the mask. Add long, dark fur to the inside corners of the ears, then make shorter fur up both inside edges. Move out to the shadows around the head itself and add dark fur texture to the brown shading all the way around.

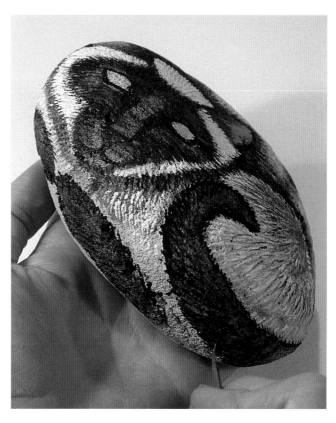

15 Continue detailing.

Lightly scatter some dark fur lines around the top of the haunch, with just a few more sprinkled about the middle portion. Several overlapping layers along the lower half of the tail for shadowing will suggest volume. Do the same along the lower half of the paws.

16 Add white fur details.

Loosen a small amount of Cloud White paint with enough water to achieve the right consistency for crisp strokes. Fan out long, delicately curving ear whiskers from the inside corners of each ear, overlapping the darker lines you made previously. Add a row of white fur below the base of the ear as well. The judicious and sparing use of white can heighten contrast in other areas, too. These areas include the edges of the head, the top curve of the haunch, the tips of the shoulders and along the edges of any other contrasting dark areas along the back. Trust your eyes to direct you to areas that would benefit from more emphasis. Several loose layers of white fur in the lower half of the haunch will brighten that area.

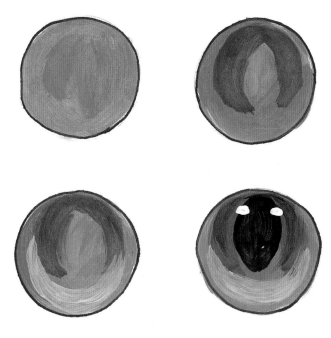

17 Paint the distinctive Siamese eyes.
Vivid blue eyes are as much the hallmark of the Siamese cat as its shaded coat and contrasting points. Select a brush suitable for filling in small, tight areas, such as a round brush in size 2 or 3. Pour out a small amount of Summer Sky Blue and matching amount of Cloud White. In a separate area, mix a brushful of each color together to get a medium blue. Fill in the almond shapes of the eyes, being careful to leave a defining outline of black surrounding them. The edges of the eyes should be as smooth and uniform as possible. If needed, you can go back after they are dry and neaten up by reapplying the black outline. Rinse your brush and take up a small amount of Summer Sky Blue. Add just enough black to get a color somewhere between royal and navy blue. Don't make it too dark or the black pupil will not show up against it. Use this to create a second, smaller half circle that extends from the top of the eye. Again rinse, then blend more white with a touch of blue to create noticeably paler shade. Form a half circle of this light blue in the lower half of the eye, leaving a narrow edge of the original blue eye color showing around the edges. When dry, add a small oval of black that hangs suspended from the top of the eye and just overlaps the highlighting half circle below. Many Siamese have crossed eyes, and should you want to paint this trait on your cat, simply move each pupil slightly off center towards the nose.

18 Accent the nose and eyes.
To warm up the face area and bring out the eyes, lighten a small amount of Woodland Brown with enough Sunflower Yellow to create a golden brown color. Apply this color with a round or flat brush, first to the bridge of the nose to pull it out from the face, then above and below each eye.

19 Accent the body.
Blot your brush and scrub this lighter brown lightly along the top portion of the haunch, avoiding the outside edges. Also, scrub behind the head and along the top edge of the face mask to create a diffused look. Add a bit of this tint into the area just below where tail and cheek meet, and any other place where it seems the fur lines could use a bit of subtle blending.

20 Add fur lines.
With a script liner, add golden brown fur lines to the top edges of the paws and tail.

21 Add whiskers.
Rinse out your brush and add one or two dots of white to the upper center of each eye. Loosen your white paint with water until the consistency is right for creating a set of long, elegant whiskers flowing out from within the muzzle area. If your whiskers get too thick, try shaving them down with an underline of dark brown. I also added a bit more dark fur to my cat's cheekbones in order to blend the edges of the highlighting there.

Create an entire Siamese family.

22 Complete a final check.
Look your cat over from every angle, searching for any areas that seem to need more detailing or defining. When you are satisfied, sign your piece and give it a sealing coat of clear acrylic to protect and enhance the colors.

More Cat Ideas

Placing two or more cats on a single rock makes for an arresting piece.

A cat sleeping on its back is another appealing pose you might want to try.

Once you've mastered the basics, you can paint any kind of cat or kitten. The cat on the far left features a second oval rock for a tail.

Cat Portraits

Here are a few recent cat portraits along with the photos I used to paint them.

How to Paint a
Dalmatian

With their dropped ears, boxy foreheads and blunt muzzles, dalmatians resemble a number of other short-haired dogs, including beagles and labrador retrievers. It's the distinctive black spots scattered all over a pure white coat that sets them apart.

1 Choose a rock.

Look for a plump rock at least 3" high (7.5cm) with a flat bottom. One side should feature an outward slope to accommodate the haunch and rear leg. A slope on the opposite side could provide space for the front paws to sprawl, but if your rock features a blunt end as mine does, you can simply tuck those front paws in under the head.

When the bottom portion of a rock curves inward, it's hard to make paws that will show, so save those rocks for something else. The surface where the head will go should be fairly smooth, while the area for the haunch may have imperfections as mine does (a small crease in the rock). If a flaw is deep or distracting, use a bit of wood filler to fill in or smooth it over.

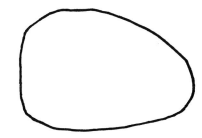

possible layouts for various rocks

2 Lay out the head.

Often I basecoat the rock first, then sketch on the design. Another option is to sketch the features first, then paint around them, leaving narrow lines uncovered to define the animal. Begin with a square head shape that takes up nearly a third of the front surface of your rock. My rock measures 6½" (16.5cm) from end to end, and my head square is 2½" (6.5cm) across. Bisect the head square horizontally. Divide the lower half in half again with a second horizontal line. Along this lower line sketch in a smaller square muzzle equal in size to one quarter of the head square. Instead of centering the muzzle, set it so that between two-thirds and three-fourths of the muzzle is to one side of the head's vertical midline, with the remaining portion on the other side. Sketch in an oval nose, setting it evenly between the side of the muzzle and the head's vertical midline.

Either freehand or using a straight edge, extend the side lines of the muzzle square up to intersect with the head's horizontal midline. Center the dog's eyes at those intersecting points. To form the bridge of the nose, angle lines from the top corners of the muzzle square to the inside edges of the eyes above. Round out the sides and bottom of the muzzle square as shown. Extend a line from the center of the nose downward to divide the muzzle, curving mouth lines off in either direction. Round off the lower half of the head square by angling lines from the middles of either side of the muzzle over to the sides of the head, cutting off the sharp corners.

From the inside corner of the eye positioned closest to the edge of the head square, extend a line straight up to the top of the head and begin one ear there. Create a line that curves up slightly from the head until it is just past the top corner of the head, then drop it down at nearly a right angle to parallel the side of the face. Stop when it is about even with the nose. Give the tip of the ear a sharp point, then bring the inside edge of the ear back up to the starting point, adding a slight outward curve to what would otherwise be an almost triangular shape. Since the dog's head is slightly turned, begin the second ear not above the second eye, but over almost to the corner of that opposite side. Slant the top of the ear down as you extend it beyond the head square until it ends level with or slightly below the tip of the first ear. Curve the inside of the ear toward the head as you bring it back up, shaving down some of the space between the eye and the original edge of the face.

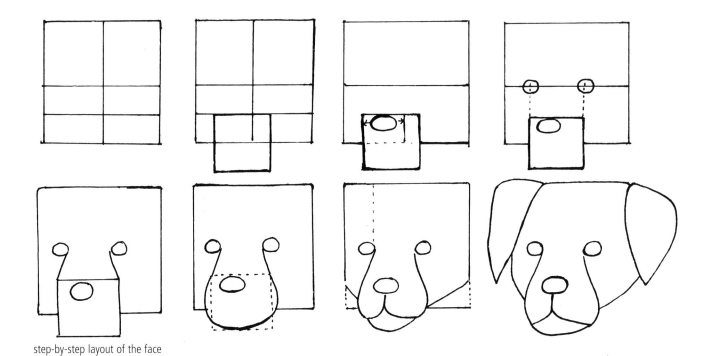

step-by-step layout of the face

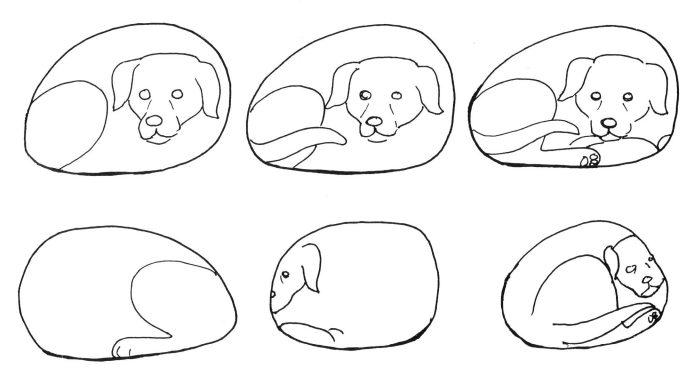

step-by-step layout of the body

3 Lay out the body.

Once the head is done, the remaining components are relatively uncomplicated. Move to the opposite end of the rock and create an oval haunch similar in size to the head, placed lengthwise. Curve a tail in from just beyond the bottom of the haunch, allowing it to angle up then droop down as it tapers to a rounded end. Fit a rear leg below the tail, shaped somewhat like an L, with a set of small oval pads showing on the paw. Use the space remaining between head and haunch to suggest a crease in the upper front leg. Give the lower leg a slight angle so that it seems to rise slightly below the head before it curves to end with a blunt paw. Bring the other front leg in from the far side like a long oval, so that the two paws almost touch near the end of the rock. Very little will show on the rear side of your rock, save for a crescent of back hip corresponding to the front one.

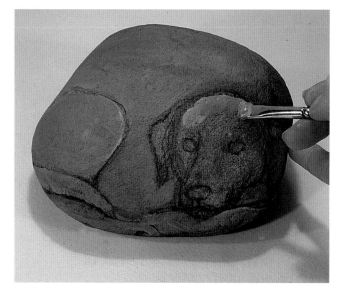

4 Paint the basecoat.

Mix one part black paint to two parts white for a medium shade of gray and use a small, stiff flat brush to cover the surface of the rock, careful not to go over the guidelines. Make sure you paint all the way to the base of the rock so that no unpainted edges show. I missed filling in the chin when applying this coat and had to do so later.

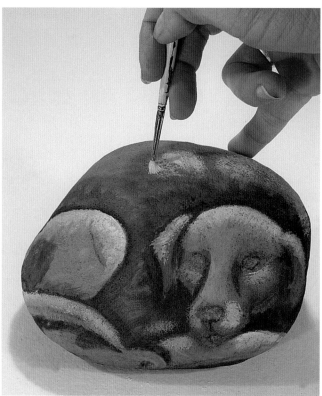

5 Create dimension with shadows.

Use the same brush and deeper gray (three parts black to one part white) to shade areas that should appear to recede, like the midsection between the head and haunch, the areas surrounding the legs and all around the head. Turn your flat brush sideways to stroke in the shadowed line running along the defining edge of the muzzle, with a shorter shadow on the corresponding side. Keep your brush rather dry by stroking excess paint onto your newspaper. Drybrushing will give your dark shadows a soft, diffused look. When shading the area beneath the muzzle, use an even darker gray—almost black—to suggest more depth and provide extra contrast for the head. On the back side of the rock you will need only to shade around the partial hip showing there. Make the tail stand out by giving it a narrow line of shadow above and below where it overlaps the haunch.

6 Add highlights.

You may use the same brush or one slightly smaller to heighten the illusion of dimension with white highlights. Again go for a diffused look, keeping your brush dry and lightly loaded. The areas that need highlighting are those that would catch light naturally; the top of the head and tops of the ears, the cheekbones below the eyes, on the muzzle at either side of the nose leather. Also, highlight the top curve of both haunches, the upper half of the tail, and the upper half of the front legs (except where the head shades a portion). Add another small smudge of highlighting to accentuate the crease above the base of the front leg. Other areas to highlight include the shoulders curving gently just beyond the shading behind the head. This area should form a soft **M** shape. Skip a space and make a second, matching swath behind the shoulders.

7 Define the facial features.

Switch to a script liner brush and mix up a tiny amount of pale pink by adding just a tip-full of Geranium Red paint to a larger drop of white. Use this color to add a sparse mustache of pink to the muzzle area directly below the nose. Rinse your brush and use straight black, loosened as needed with water, to fill in the nose leather. Outline the shape of the mouth and the eye circles, too, adding small corners at the lower inside and upper outside points. For the eyes, darken a tiny drop of Patio Brick with just enough black to create a dark, chocolate brown and use this to fill in both eye circles.

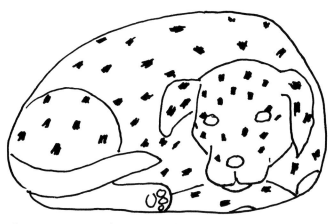

these spots are too uniform in size and placement

8 Add the spots.

Use a small round or worn-down flat brush to begin dappling your dog with its pattern of spots. Avoid symmetry by placing some spots in random clusters of twos and threes. Start at the head with smaller spots that vary in shape and size. Make the ear spots larger, perhaps even partially covering one of the ears. Then, work your way backwards, adding spots in the shadowed areas as well as along the highlighted features. Try to let the shape of the spots suggest the shape of the underlying body parts, so that they seem to curve slightly where the dog's haunch is curved, or are partially hidden from view atop the dog's head.

these spots correspond to underlying contours

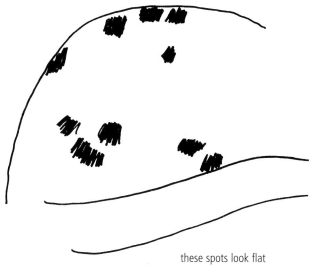

these spots look flat

9 Create fur texture.

At this point your Dalmatian is still more black and gray than black and white, but against a darker background, short, white fur will stand out more clearly than white-on-white fur would. To make the delicate, splinter strokes for short fur, you will need to adjust the consistency of your paint. Add small increments of water to white paint and mix until it is loose enough to flow smoothly off the tip of your script liner brush, without running or turning transparent as it dries. Test strokes on newspaper will help you check for the right balance of paint and water. Also, holding your brush almost perpendicular to the surface and using just the tip will keep your fur crisply defined. Begin by detailing the sides of the face with the shortest and most delicate of strokes set as closely together as you can make them. Accent the eyes by encircling them with white outlines just beyond the black ones, and give the chin a fringe of fur. Next fill in the interior of the face with more layers of small strokes, following the fur direction guide. Avoid obliterating the darker lines defining the muzzle or the bridge of the nose. Interior fur strokes need not be as dense as those used along the outer edges, but they should still be short and delicate, and done in overlapping layers for a seamless look. On the ears, the fur should be densest at the tops and more sparse along the lower portions. Remember that fur tends to grow outward away from the nose, so when you reach a black spot, detail it with a fringe of white fur along the edge closest to the nose. Later you can detail the far sides of the spots with black fur strokes.

In areas that are deeply shadowed, allow more distance between each fur stroke so that the overall impression of shadowing still shows through under a light layer of fur. For areas that should be lighter, like the upper bridge of the nose, your strokes can be so close and dense as to nearly appear solid white. Along the muzzle, stroke sideways to suggest several rows of whisker follicles there.

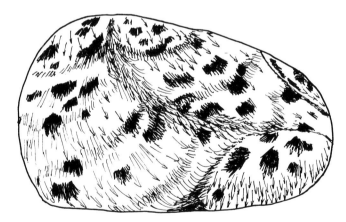

fur direction guide

10 Detail the haunch.

As with the face, begin by outlining the entire outer edge with very dense splinter strokes, then fill in the interior, again clustering more strokes in highlighted areas while making them sparser as you work down into the shadowed areas. Add a fringe of texture to the sides of the spots indicating the direction the fur is growing, which on the haunch would be the top side.

11 Detail the shoulders and back.

To detail the shoulders and backside, it's helpful to turn the rock so you can stroke toward yourself rather than away. Concentrate your strokes in those areas you previously highlighted, spacing the strokes farther apart in shadowy areas before dwindling away altogether to leave a dark margin for contrast. Detail the spots along the sides facing the head. Now move down, curving your sets of

strokes in wide crescents to suggest the gentle curve of the dog's body in the direction of the tail. This curving is also reflected in the changing direction of the detailing fringe along the edge of the spots, so consult the fur direction illustration for guidance. Remember to make your fur lines more sparse as you near the bottom edge of the rock where it would naturally be more shadowed. Leave a darker spine line in place down the center of the back.

12 Complete the fur.

Turn your rock around again, and work on detailing the remaining unfinished areas. The fur surrounding the head tends to radiate out from it like sunrays. Don't stroke too far into the shadowy margins needed to set off the head and define other elements such as that small crease above the base of the front leg. To give the chest a bit more volume, add an extra dense few rows of strokes surrounding the face just beyond the ear.

Next move to the front leg, making the fur very short and dense along the top edge, except where the head overlaps it. Handle the tail in a similar fashion, leaving the bottom half mostly shaded. The rear leg is also detailed mainly along the top, with the fur becoming sparser in the middle with only a bit of broken line along the bottom edge.

13 Detail the nose.

To give the nose detail and dimension, add two white, C-shaped nostril holes like reversed parentheses. Soften the white paint to pale gray and create a gleam across the top of the nose just below the edge.

14 Detail the eyes.

I used black paint to tidy up the outer eye, then reapplied the white outline and gave the inside eye a tiny corner of white. To complete the eyes, use straight black paint to create an oval shaped pupil near the top of each eye. With a tiny amount of Patio Brick on the brush tip, add a narrow crescent of reddish-brown inside the bottom half of each eye. One or two white dots in the pupils will give your dalmatian's eyes a lifelike gleam.

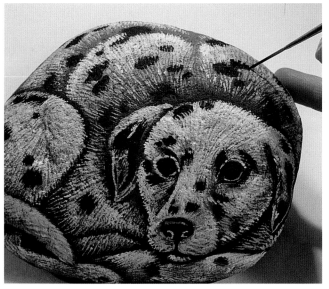

15 Detail the spots.

I used black to add touches of fringe to the backsides of my spots wherever I thought they needed the extra definition.

16 Finish paws.

Making the rear foot's paw pads pink would adds a welcome bit of color to the piece. Mix a touch of red into a drop of white paint and fill in the centers of each individual pad, leaving a border of gray surrounding them.

17 Finish the tail.

In looking over my dog, I felt that the tail needed more definition, so I used dark gray to stroke in some additional fur texture just where the tail overlaps the haunch. Work at training your eye to see areas that are not clearly defined or that lack needed contrast. Developing that judgment is part of your ongoing growth as an artist.

How to Paint an
Irish Setter

An Irish setter's rich russet coat, splashed with fiery highlights, makes this dog a striking subject. Changing coat colors will allow you to paint other kinds of setters as well. With minor modifications you can also create golden retrievers, cocker spaniels, collies and a host of other long-haired dogs. Rendering the flowing or feathery coat of a long-haired dog requires a slightly different technique than that used for short-haired dogs.

What You'll Need

- DecoArt Patio Paint in Geranium Red, Wrought Iron Black, Patio Brick, Sunshine Yellow, Sunflower Yellow, Cloud White
- assorted stiff, flat brushes
- no. 4 or 6 round brush
- 1/4" Silver Brush Ruby Satin Grass Comb
- Loew-Cornell script liner, no. 1
- white charcoal pencil
- spray acrylic sealer

1 Choose a rock.

When selecting a rock, look for a plump oval, preferably with a slight angle at one end suggesting the crook of the rear leg. Your rock can be fairly high, almost loaf-shaped or merely rounded on top. The rock I selected is 7" (18cm) long, 5" (12.5cm) across and just under 3" (7.5cm) high. If my rock had a side that was flat enough to stand up on, I could have opted for a more upright pose, but avoid rocks so tall and round that your dog will seem to be arching its back. Scrub your rock and allow it to dry. Sketching the dog's features on in pencil is a good way to experiment and see how best to fit them to your particular rock.

2 Paint the basecoat.

Mix up enough paint to cover the entire visible surface of your rock, using two parts Geranium Red to one part black to get a very deep reddish-brown. Apply with a large flat brush, slightly dampened. Allow the paint to dry.

two parts red, one part black (Irish setter basecoat)

black with a trace of red

two parts Sunshine Yellow, one part Patio Brick and one part red

two parts Sunshine Yellow and one part Patio Brick

two parts red and one part Patio Brick

Sunflower Yellow

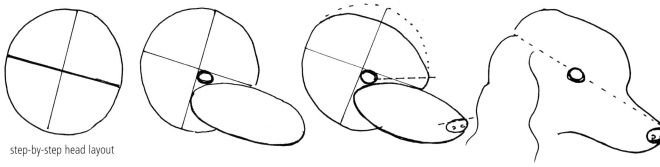

step-by-step head layout

3 Sketch the features.

Because setters have drooping ears, head placement can be higher on the rock as though the dog's head is raised. Consider how much space your rock has for the ear, which will splay out at the end if the head is low. My rock's side curves in slightly near the base, making a splayed ear difficult to render, so I opted for a slightly raised head. With a white charcoal pencil, sketch a circle for the head. This circle should be placed to one side of the rock, but with room beyond the outside edge to fit the ear. On my 7" (18cm) rock, the head circle measures 2¹/₂" (6.5cm), or approximately one-third of the rock's length. In this case, the head is tilted down, so I bisected the head circle with a line that slants toward the center of the rock. I then bisected the rock in the opposite direction, forming a cross. The muzzle is a large, elongated oval. Begin the oval in the lower inside quarter of the head circle and extend it until equal parts are inside and outside of the head. The muzzle's length should be the same as the diameter of the head and wide enough to nearly fill the space of that quarter. Fit the eye into the center corner of that same quarter. A straight line from the eye circle to a corresponding point just above where the top of the muzzle oval crosses the head circle indicates where a second, unseen eye would be. Use this same straight line as a guide while sketching a small oval nose into the upper end of the muzzle. The top of the nose oval should be set on a line parallel to that of the eyes above it. This will help you avoid a skewed look. The same point where the eye line crosses the head circle also indicates where to begin modifying the head shape. Just above the unseen eye, shave off the entire top curve so that the head is flattened. For a cocker spaniel, leave the head a rounded dome. Add the ear, beginning inside the head circle at a point that lines up with the top of the nose and the center of the eye circle. From the base of the ear allow the outermost ear line to gently curve out and away from the head as the fur flows gracefully downward. My dog's ear measures ³/₄" (2cm) across the top.

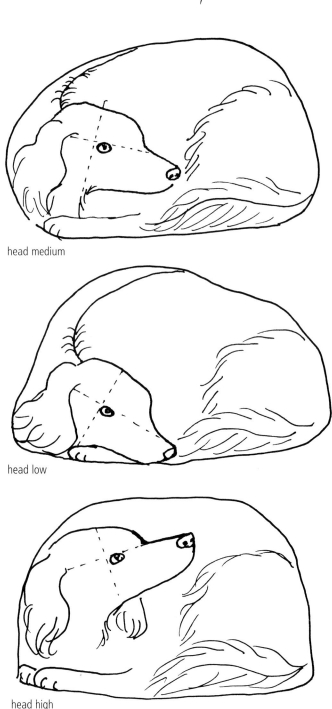

head medium

head low

head high

4 Finish the layout.

To complete your layout, bring a sweeping plume of a tail in from the base at the opposite end of the rock, allowing the tip to taper off below the dog's head. Add a narrow front leg that begins where the tail tip ends, fitting the paw below the chest. Sketch a spine line that curves out from behind the head just above the base of the ear. Allow this spine line to follow the contour of your rock until it ends at the base of the tail. Above the tail, indicate the curve of a haunch similar in size to the head (measured from nose to base of ear). Look your sketch over to see how all the elements fit together. Double-check to ensure that the nose and eyes are parallel.

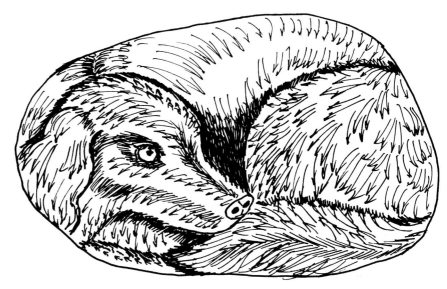

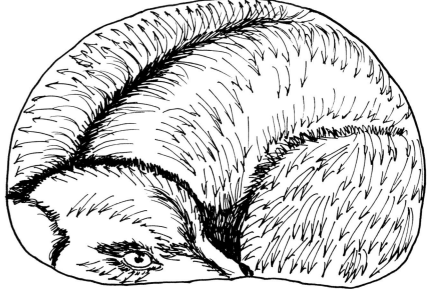

fur direction guide

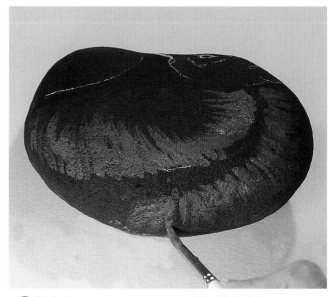

5 Create contours with shading.

For dimension and depth, use black paint, softened with just a trace amount of Geranium Red, to darken the areas surrounding the head, haunch, and the space between these two features. Go around the tail, ear and down the spine. Use a round brush or the side of a flat one to feather out the edges of your shadows, avoiding harsh contrasts. Shade the center portion of the setter's tail to indicate a natural part in the fur there.

6 Heighten the contours with highlights.

Highlights suggest the dramatic play of light over the dog's fur, emphasizing the shape of features and adding subtle texture. Again using a round brush, the side of a flat one, or a grass comb for the larger areas, mix two parts Sunshine Yellow with one part red and one part Patio Brick. Add just enough water to ensure smooth application. Begin on the backside, stroking a line of curving highlights along either side of the darkened spine line. Nestle each stroke up against the previous one, but allow them to separate as they taper to points. These strokes should grow longer as you proceed toward the tail end. Consult the fur direction guide, and end the strokes well before reaching the top of the haunch. Leave the dog's midsection mostly dark for now.

Turn your rock around and use slightly more diluted paint to suggest a silkier sheen along the top of the head. Leave the center of the muzzle dark all the way up between the eyes and into the forehead. Add a softly blended line of highlighting just below this dark swath, moving first over the top of the eye, then down and around the bottom to encircle it, while leaving a dark oval of basecoat surrounding the eye itself. Return to more concentrated paint to suggest several layers of fur flowing like ripples down the ear. Use the tip of your brush to create a series of short ragged lines along the jaw line and neck.

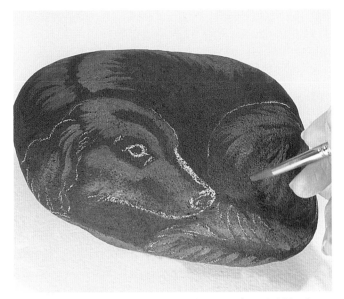

Softly highlight along the top of the front leg. Add high-lights along the tail similar to those made along either side of the spine line. More feathery strokes add detail to the haunch. Concentrate them just below the top curve, then scatter them more randomly, but in the direction the fur would naturally flow as indicated by the fur direction guide.

7 Outline the eyes and nose.
While the highlights are drying, switch to a script liner and black paint to outline around the nose, fill in the nostrils and outline the eye.

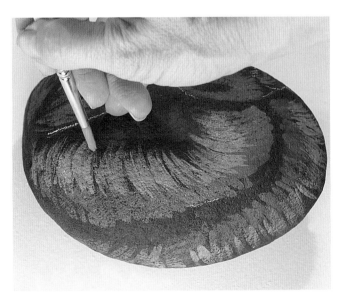

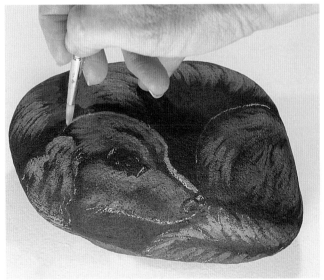

8 Add a layer of light and texture.
Mix two parts Sunshine Yellow with one part Patio brick to create a tone visibly brighter than the previous color. Use the tip of your round brush or a grass comb to create an overlapping, somewhat ragged row of strokes that begin where your first set of spine highlights left off, again allowing the tips of the strokes to separate. Try for a more soft, diffused look, holding your brush perpendicular to the surface.

From there, concentrate lighter strokes along the top half of the tail and then the haunch in a rather random fash-ion. Do more highlighting on the ear, mainly around the top where light would fall first. Add a narrow line of pale golden color to the very top of the muzzle to make it stand out. Continue along the top of the head, using the lighter tone to visually set the head off from the body.

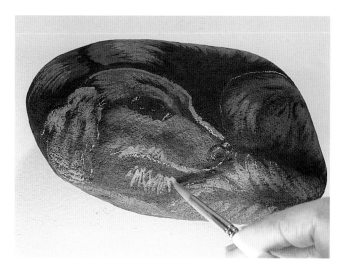

Similarly, bring out the jaw line by blending a ragged row of fur into the darker highlights there. Make a smoother outline along the bottom of the muzzle ending near the nose. To keep the area directly below the head from seeming bottomless, add a ruff of coarse fur to the center, leaving the surrounding edges of the area dark.

9 Add delicate fur details.

Continuing with the same color, switch to your script liner brush (or, if your rock is smooth, try using your grass comb) to create clusters of fur lines that are dense, but thin and much more delicate than those previously done. Adjust the consistency of your paint so that it is almost like ink. Leave a margin of darker basecoat showing, then drop down below the second set of highlighting strokes along the dog's midsection between head and haunch. Note how narrow, yet distinct, dark margins around all main features help to define them. As you add these longer, more delicate lines, curve them in small clusters that suggest waviness. Allow some lines to cross others here and there. Move next to the top and side of the haunch, concentrating these fine fur lines to emulate the way light would fall on the curved roundness of the haunch. Make fewer and more sparse strokes in the lower portions.

On the head, use your script liner brush to create much shorter and more dense fur, adding texture and light to the top of the head, to the highlighted parts of the muzzle, and around the eyes, jaw line and ear. Along the muzzle in particular, make overlapping rows of short splinter strokes rather than longer ones. A fringe of short, diagonal lines along the inside edge of the ear near the top is another nice detail.

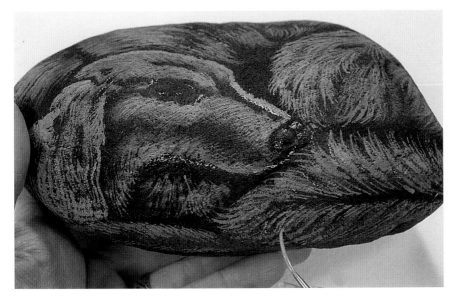

Along the top of the front leg, create a series of very short, very uniform strokes, like a slanted row of splinters whose tips show up dramatically against the dark basecoat above. On the tail, these lines add realistic texture and visual interest, but use them sparingly so that the subtle interplay of previous layers of color show through.

10 Accent the highlights.

Now mix one part Patio Brick with two parts red and, still using a script liner, go back over your animal's coat, adding a scattering of this deeper reddish-brown to both complement and accent the lighter highlights. Use them to soften and blend the areas where darker and lighter fur strokes adjoin, such as along the spine. In the space below the head, the lighter ruff looks a bit stark against the dark basecoat. Deep red fur lines can create a more natural transition. Other places to use it include the dark oval surrounding the eye, down the center line of the muzzle and in the middle of the forehead. Avoid diminishing the highlights by keeping these red strokes very sparse.

11 Fill in the eyes.

Mix Patio Brick and Sunshine Yellow to get a warm golden brown. Use this and your script liner brush to fill in the eye circle, leaving the center dark. Add a touch of black to your eye color and create a small crescent of shadow within the top half of the eye. When dry, add an oval, black pupil that hangs from the top of the eye.

12 Detail the eyes and nose.

Add a bit of black to a drop of white paint to make a soft gray, and underline the bottom half of the eye just outside its black outline. Deepen this gray with more black and add a tiny amount of red to create the dark pinkish-gray tone of the nose leather. Use it to surround each nostril, leaving a dark line between them. Then, add white to make a highlighting color and use the very tip of your liner to create a narrow half circle gleam above and below each nostril.

13 Detail the coat with yellow.

In looking over my dog's coat, I determined that it could use one more layer of highlighting to heighten the look of shimmering fire. I used straight Sunflower Yellow and my script liner to sprinkle a few bright touches among the areas previously highlighted. It's easy to overlook places that are tucked out of the way, like the front leg, but highlighting the fur along the top really helps define it.

The addition of one or two white dots to the eye gives your painted dog the look of a live dog suddenly watching you.

How to Paint a
Bulldog

Bulldogs, pugs, Boston terriers and Pekingese may not win conventional beauty contests, but to their devotees these stout little canines have charms that far outweigh their homeliness. Often they are described as being so ugly they're cute.

For rock painters, the obvious advantage is that, with no muzzle to speak of, bulldogs and other flat-faced dogs fit easily onto an array of rock shapes, most particularly round rocks that are not suitable for most other subjects.

1 Choose a rock.

When selecting your rock, look for chubby ones that are circular or oval, but with one flatter side to serve as the base. Rounded rocks with a higher profile can be employed for sitting poses. The most important consideration is a broad area where the face, with its generous jowls, dewlaps and widely spaced eyes, will fit. The hindquarters seem petite by comparison, so if your round rock tapers at one end, so much the better. The rock I selected is fairly uniform, yet not perfectly round, and about the size of a small melon. From end to end it measures 7" (18cm) and it is 5¹/₂" (14cm) wide. The end I chose for the head had a small crack slightly off center that I filled in with a bit of wood filler.

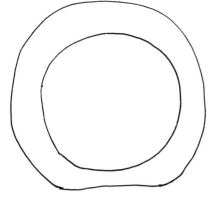
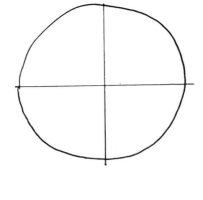
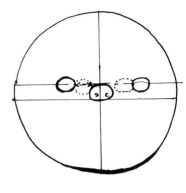

step-by-step head layout

2 Lay out the head.

Because these dogs have massive heads, begin by sketching in a circle that takes up approximately one-third of the total area of the rock you've chosen. On my 7" (18cm) rock, the diameter of the head circle is 5" (12.5cm) and covers most of one end of my rock. Placement may vary depending on the contours of your particular rock, but do try to leave space below the head circle to tuck two front paws.

Bisect the head circle both horizontally and vertically, then place an oval nose so that it is in the center resting atop the horizontal midline. Next make a second horizontal line that runs across the top of the nose oval. Center the eye circles on this line, with a space equal to the diameter of an eye circle between it and the nose.

Below the nose, extend a short line down the vertical bisecting line, then split it into two diverging mouth lines that curve sharply sideways until each

is well past being even with the outside edge of the nose oval. Curve the mouth lines downward from there, angling them slightly away from each other. When you reach the bottom edge of the head circle, form a curved jowl. Depending on your rock, these jowls may even droop slightly beyond the head circle. They should then loop back up and run parallel to the inside mouth/jowl lines, before curving in just below the eye circles to join above the nose oval.

The ears are small flaps slightly indented into the head circle and set so that the base of either ear lines up with the outside edge of the eye below. Make a **J**-shaped line curving out beyond the head circle and dropping down along side it until the tip is even with the first horizontal bisecting line.

Go back to the mouth lines below the nose and indicate a bottom lip below them. Holding a pencil level with the eyes is a simple way to check for symmetry.

3 Layout the body.

Below the jowls, leave a small open space. Then, sketch in two stubby round paws at the ends of equally stubby legs curving in from either side. Fit the ends of the paws with a set of four oval toes and four pointy little toenails. Turn your rock sideways and create an elbow and short upper leg as shown. At the rear of the rock on either side, create a round haunch that is one-third to one-half the size of the head, with elongated back paws extending from the bottom. Finish the feet by adding three small curving toes. The tail can either be a short, docked stub or a thick, tapered tail that curves off to one side. That completes your basic layout.

4 Paint the brown patches.

Markings vary from dog to dog, and color patches range from dark blond to deep brown to brindle and every shade in between. My choice is a medium shade of brown concentrated in a saddle shape on the back and sides, along with the upper half of the head. Use Pinecone Brown and a large flat brush to cover the back, sides and rear portion of the haunches. I also left a narrow space around the front of each haunch to be painted white along with the bottom of the midsection surrounding the rear feet. Paint the top of the head, leaving a narrow blaze unpainted above the nose.

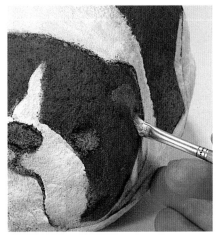

6 **Fill in the ears.**
Mix a tiny amount of red into white paint to get a medium shade of pink. Add just a touch of black to soften the pink to a dusky shade and use this to paint the insides of the ears.

7 **Paint the facial features.**
Switch to black paint and a script liner to outline the nose, mouth/jowl and eyes. Fill in the entire space above the bottom lip, then add enough water to your paint to thin it almost to transparency, and stroke a ragged row of vertical lines below the bottom lip to a little beyond halfway to the bottoms of the jowls.

8 **Add some facial details.**
Mix enough black into Patio Brick to get a dark chocolate brown. Use a script liner to go around the outlines of the jowls with tiny splinter strokes. Change the angles of these strokes in relation to the nose—they should radiate out like sunrays. Create the same delicate fringe around the ear edges to define their shapes in a furry way.

9 **Define the features with outlines.**
For a bolder outline that also can be accomplished more quickly, select a stiff, flat craft brush. Add water to your dark brown mixture and do some short test strokes that are little more than pressing the brush down then picking it up again with only enough drag to create the suggestion of texture. Repeat this stroke in a line along the top of the head, then skip down to the edges of the face and do the same, always pulling your brush away from the line you're emphasizing.

Use scant paint and a dry brush to scrub black paint into smudgy shadows below the jowls.

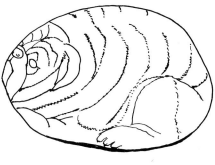
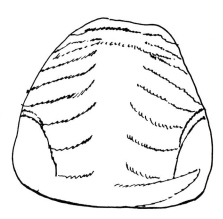

placement of dewlaps, wrinkles and folds

10 Paint some wrinkles and folds.

Add a small amount of Patio Brick to your black paint. Between the eyes, create two short, curved lines that begin above either side of the nose and end by curving into the eye cir- cles halfway across. Make a second set of parallel curves that begin inside the first set and end beyond the outside corner of either eye. Another set of wrinkles start near the bottom of the jowl on either side and curve up to below the ear. These end in the center of the forehead. Make two more shorter wrinkles, one below and one above the ones you just made. Indicate a small, sagging line under either eye. Between the jowls and front paws, paint in a pair of curved dewlaps.

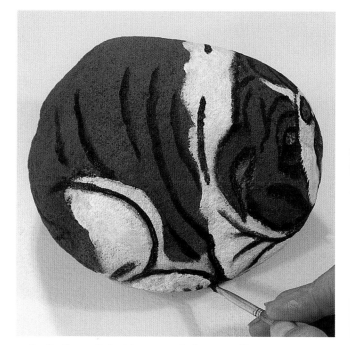

11 Complete the remaining outlines.

Go over the leg outlines and creases. Create a series of wrinkles or fold lines around the head and along the sides. Break off those nearest the head before they meet at the top of the back. Also, go around the haunch, rear leg and foot.

From the rear, outline the tail as it curves around one side, or outline the stub if the tail is docked.

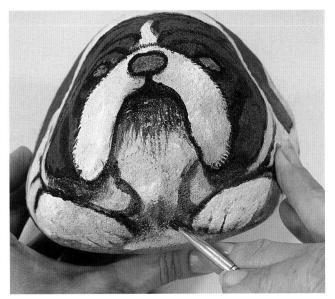

12 **Shadow dewlaps and paws.**
Use black and a dry brush to create shadows below the dew laps and between paws.

13 **Highlight the brown folds.**
Mix Pinecone Brown and Sunflower Yellow to get a warm blond color. Use a stiff, flat brush and keep it dry, applying paint along the tops of the folds then scrubbing it into the middles for a soft, diffused look.

Do the same soft highlighting along the tops of the folds along the dog's backside, blending the lighter color into the darker basecoat. Highlight along the top side of the tail, too.

14 **Detail the white patch behind the head.**
Mix white and black paint to get a medium gray. Loosen with water and use your script liner to make a fringe of gray fur lines behind the head. Keep your strokes delicate but dense, and intersperse with longer strokes. Work all the way around the head, keeping these fur lines perpendicular to the line they are shadowing. When the head is done, detail any folds in the white patch behind the head.

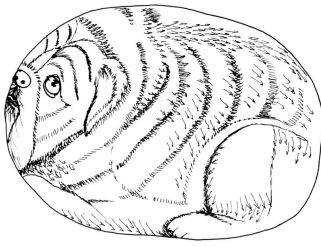

fur direction guide

15 **Detail the muzzle and jowls.**
Still using gray paint, create several sets of shallow, U-shaped rows of fine fur lines in the lower jaw area between the jowls, slightly above where they end. Next move to the muzzle and begin with a narrow curving line to either side of the nose, running parallel to the drooping lines of the mouth but stopping when each side is less than halfway down the jowl. Go back over these lines with splinter strokes. Below this first set of muzzle lines, make a second and third set, each a little longer and having a slightly different angle. Dilute your paint so that it is just a bit thinner and add one more lighter set of these muzzle lines, then darken the area below the nose. Also, use this thinner gray paint to soften the edges of the mouth lines.

16 **Add details to white areas.**
Adding realistic details to all the remaining white areas can be done in two basic steps. First, use delicate gray fur lines to create the look of shadows on the lower sides of any feature. This means along the bottom curve of the front legs, along the lower edge of the rear legs, the lower edges of the haunches and along the bottom of any space showing between the rear paw and the front leg. Use lighter gray strokes to suggest milder shadows where one feature might overlap another, such as below the head or along the lower edges of the white folds. When you've completed this shadowing, switch to white paint that's been loosened enough to create delicate details, and begin adding a fringe of white fur to any edge where white fur meets brown.

How to Paint a Bulldog

17 Add details to the brown areas.

In the same way, but with a different color, add fur texture to the folds and wrinkles in your dog's brown areas. Mix enough Sunflower Yellow into your white paint to get a discernably lighter shade. Use your script liner and your most delicate fur strokes to add texture to the areas previously highlighted. Begin with the head, detailing not only the top edges of the folds, but also the outside edges of the head and the angles of the ears.

18 Soften the edges further.

When the head is completed, move on to the rest of the body, using your highlighting fur lines to further soften the edges where lighter color was scrubbed on earlier, as well as to give the back portions the look of real fur. Don't overlook the brown portions of the haunches or the top half of the tail.

19 Integrate the fur lines on the spine.

Mix up another small batch of dark brown by adding a brushful of black to a puddle of Patio Brick. Use this deeper brown to further integrate the fur lines along the back. Concentrate on the layers of fur down the center of the back where the spine runs to the base of the tail. Next, use these dark strokes to soften the edges of the folds along both sides of the back plus those that run down into the midsections between front and rear legs.

Once the back is completed, move to the face and use these dark fur lines to soften the face folds and wrinkles.

20 **Detail the eyes and nose.**
Fill in the eye circles with straight Pinecone Brown, then add a crescent of Sunflower Yellow to the lower half of each eye as a highlight. While the eyes are drying, color in the nose leather with solid black.

21 **Finish the eyes, nose and mouth.**
Now add a black pupil to the upper center of each eye. Mix up a paler shade of gray, and use this on your script liner to create a gleam across the top of the nose and a pair of half-round nostrils. Also, use this gray to paint in the barest suggestion of a gleam to the upper half of the lower lip, and a longer gleam along the bottom of the lower lip. Add a scattering of gray fur lines to the chin area, too. Then, with the very tip of your brush, make narrow curves of gray below each eye, letting the curves sag toward the outside edges to give the eyes a droopy look.

22 **Add the final touches.**
Small white gleams in each eye have a powerful impact on this piece. As an afterthought, I added a narrow defining line of lightened Sunflower Yellow to the eyelid to give the eyes a bit more emphasis.

In looking over my bulldog, I decided that adding a blush of pink to the front toes would be a nice touch. I mixed up a very pale shade of pink from Geranium Red and white and used a dry brush to simply scrub the color onto the toes. A light spray of sealer will make all your colors seem richer.

How to Paint a Bulldog   243

How to Paint a
Yorkie

Yorkshire terriers are among the most popular of those tiny dogs bred as lap pets. With their shoe-button eyes and lively dispositions, plus an elegant cascade of silky fur, it's easy to see why people find Yorkies irresistible companions.

Not surprisingly, rock Yorkies are adorable, too. To paint your own, look for tombstone-shaped rock that will stand up on a flat end. Yorkies can also be painted on narrow, loaf-shaped rocks.

What You'll Need

- DecoArt Patio Paint in Wrought Iron Black, Cloud White, Sunflower Yellow, Patio Brick, Daisy Cream, Sunshine Yellow (or other bow color of your choice)
- assorted stiff, flat brushes including one ³/₄" or larger
- no. 4 or 6 round
- Silver Brush Ruby Satin Grass Comb (optional)
- Loew-Cornell script liner, no. 1
- graphite pencil
- Sharpie marker (optional)
- spray acrylic sealer

1 Choose a rock.
The rock I found for this project stands just under 7" (18cm) high and tapers slightly at the top. Avoid rocks that are so pointy that the two ears at the top can not be at least one ear-width apart. Adequate height for upright ears is also an important consideration, and my rock, being rounded at the top and almost 4" (10cm)

thick, allows ample room for them, although the tips will lay across the top of the rock. This means my finished piece will look best when viewed from above. Yorkies' coats are often clipped into shorter layers, but those that participate in dog shows sport long, luxuriant show coats that flow down to the floor.

lots of ear room   minimal ear room   not enough ear room

2 Sketch the features.

Begin by determining how the triangular ears can best fit your rock. If your rock is very thin along the top, it may not be feasible to wrap the ears around the curve there. In that case, begin the base of the ears lower down, and fill the center between the two ears with a taller sprout of pulled-back facial hair gathered into a little bow. On thicker rocks there is more room to maneuver, and ears can begin closer to the top of the front surface.

On my 7" (18cm) tall rock, the head is a 3" (7.5cm) circle with the bases of the ears slightly indented within it. Bisect the head circle horizontally and fit a second, smaller circle for the muzzle into the lower half as shown. Bisect this muzzle circle horizontally, too, indicating a mouth line. Along this mouth line sketch in a small, curved bottom lip, and below that a slightly broader chin crescent. Halfway between the mouth line and the top of the muzzle circle, sketch in a small oval nose.

Place the eyes so they rest along the horizontal midline, two full eye widths apart. The dog's eyes should not be overly large. On my dog they measure barely ¹/₂" (13mm) across.

Imagine how the fur around the eyes would be drawn up into a bow between the ears. It would follow a straight line up from the nose, while fur above the eyes would have to curve around the base of the ears.

The fur surrounding the muzzle and below the eyes should flow in loose parallel lines along either side of that circle, curving in slightly below the chin, then continuing in wavy lines down to the base of the rock.

Turn your rock to the side and make wavy lines to indicate the outside edges of the dog's mane as it flows from behind (or above) the ears and downward somewhat parallel to the curves of the lines around and down from the muzzle.

Make wavy lines to indicate the outside edges of the dog's mane as it flows from behind (or above) the ears and downward somewhat parallel to the curves of the lines around and down from the muzzle.

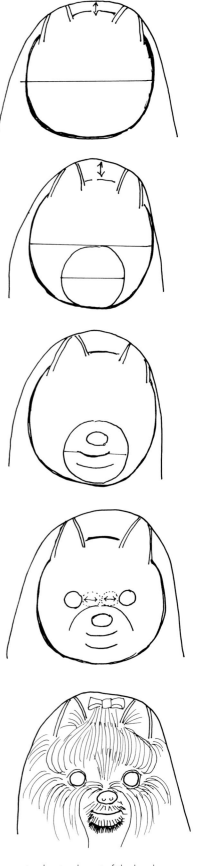

body layout

step-by-step layout of the head

fur direction guide

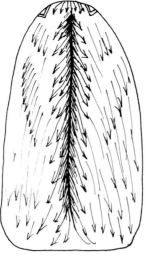

Here's my rock with the sketch in place.

color samples for mane

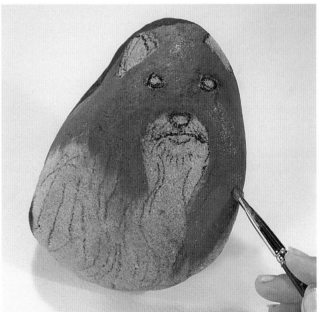

3 Paint the basecoat.

Use a large, flat brush and black paint to completely cover the back half of your rock, being careful to go around the tips of the ears if they protrude beyond the head. Paint all the way to the base of your rock so no uncovered surface can be seen.

4 Paint the mane.

To paint the mane, begin with a large puddle of Patio Brick and darken with just enough black paint to get a rich reddish-brown color. You may want to use a slightly smaller flat brush to apply this paint. Cover the entire mane area, leaving only the eyes, ears, the muzzle and the center of the chest below it unpainted.

How to Paint a Yorkie

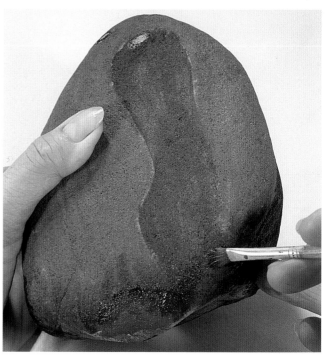

Next, add even more black paint to your mixture, turning it into a deep, chocolate brown. Use this color to fill in the ear triangles as well as the muzzle and remaining chest area. If you're worried about covering over your mouth and chin lines, simply paint around them, or go over them with a sharpie marker that will show through all but the heaviest of paints.

Tilt your rock and add dark crescents along the very bottom to suggest the curved tops of two front paws peeking from below the fur there.

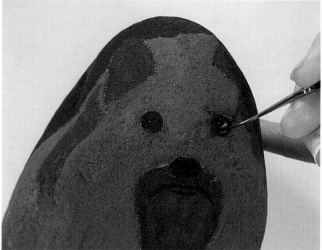

Finally, just below the ears along either side, paint a dark streak that follows the contours of the mane and tapers to a point that's level with the height of the chin.

5 Paint the facial features.
Switch to a script liner and straight black paint. Carefully outline around the shapes of the eyes, making them as round and symmetrical as you can. Also, outline and fill in the nose oval and paint over the mouth lines. Note how I added short slanting lines to either end of my upper mouth line.

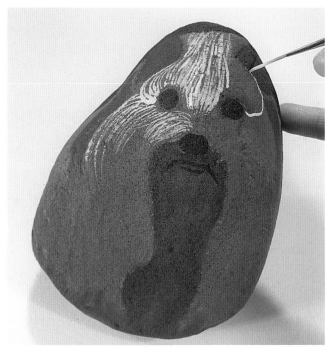

6 Create a flowing mane.

Combine white paint with enough Sunflower Yellow to make a pale, creamy gold. Add sufficient water to the paint so it will flow smoothly off the tip of your script liner, without being so watery that it runs or turns transparent. Leaving a narrow margin of basecoat in place, begin at the outside corner of either eye. Stroke in a set of narrow lines that curve out nearly as far as the outside edge of the ear, then circle back to run along the base of the ear to the inside corner, ending at the top of the head. Each successive line will be less curved as you work around the top of each eye. Between the eyes these lines should begin level with the bottoms of the eyes and extend up to the top of the head.

7 Detail the lower mane.

To detail the lower portion of the face and the rest of the flowing mane, start by making a curved row of lines along either side of the top of the muzzle. Leave a narrow margin between these muzzle lines and the row of lines beginning between the eyes above. In the same way, leave a narrow part showing down the center of the muzzle. Also, leave narrow margins of basecoat showing around the bottom edges of each eye as you surround them with fur strokes. The first few sets can be a few inches long, then begin pulling out longer lines that mirror the undulating curves of the mane all the way to the bottom of the rock. I made my lines denser at the tops of a curve, then sparser below, adding to the look of waviness. Keep my fur lines sparse over the dark shadows below either ear.

8 Detail below the nose and along the chest.

Lighten Patio Brick with a bit of Sunflower Yellow and use this color to add prickly texture to the lower portion of the muzzle. Surround the bottom half of the nose with short, bristling strokes, then make several layers of longer strokes to either side, following the shape of the mouth. Separate these strokes from the flowing fur of the mane. Skip down to the chest below the chin and make overlapping sets of long fur lines down until they feather out near the bottom. Again, leave margins of the darker basecoat undetailed to either side for contrast.

9 Outline the ears.
While you have this same reddish-gold color, use it to outline the edges of the ears, leaving narrow margins of darker color around the outlines wherever possible.

10 Outline the eyes.
Mix a tiny amount of black into Patio Brick to darken it, then add just enough white to get a creamy reddish-beige. Use this color to outline your eyes, leaving the inside lower corners open, and giving the outside upper edge a slight crimp. To further emphasize the eyes, mix some dark brown from Patio Brick and black, and go around the outside edges of the beige outlines.

11 Add more highlights.
Switch to Daisy Cream, again adjusting the texture of the paint by adding water until it flows smoothly without being too watery. Use this lighter color to complement and emphasize the fur lines surrounding the face and mane. Concentrate these strokes to suggest the play of light between and above the eyes and along the wavy curves of the mane, skipping over the more shaded areas. This will play up the contrast between lighter and darker fur. In particular, highlight the strands of fur along either side of the darker chest area, again to heighten contrast. Move to the bridge of the nose and, along either side of the darkened center, create pale, stiff fur that bristles up and out, with some delicate tips even arching up into the corners of the eyes.

12 Add details to the mouth and ears.

To a small amount of Daisy Cream, add a brushful of Patio Brick and another brushful of Sunflower Yellow. Use this light reddish-gold color and the very tip of your liner brush to fill in the narrow chin area below the mouth with very short, fine fur. Add a bit of water to loosen the paint, then use it to stroke in a cluster of ear whiskers that fan out from the inside corners.

13 Add contrasting strokes to the muzzle and chest.

Mix Patio Brick with black to get a dark brown color and, still using your script liner, stroke in delicate muzzle fur lines which radiate outward from the nose in short over-lapping layers. Move down to the area below the chin and use shorter, denser strokes to suggest shading and create depth there. Scatter longer, sparser strokes down the chest area, also using them to heighten contrast along side the pale edges of the mane.

14 Tint the fur.

Add more Patio Brick to your mixture to make a reddish-brown color, then water it down until it is a transparent tint strong enough to color lighter areas but too weak to cover anything up. Use a medium-sized round or flat brush to apply this tint above and below the eyes so that the underlying texture of the fur still shows through, yet is softened. Note how this tinting is highest above the inside corner of the eye, then tapers toward the outside end, while underneath it is narrow along the inside corners, then widens before tapering off below the outside edges of the eyes.

15 Detail and emphasize the mane.

Next, stroke off excess tint onto a paper towel or newspaper. Scrub what remains on your brush into those areas of the mane not highlighted, to warm up and tone down the fur strokes and emphasize the look of waviness. Add a few strokes of this tint to the forehead, mostly near the top.

16 Finish the face.

Mix black and white to make a medium gray color. Use the tip of your script liner to make two small, half-round lines indicating nostrils in the lower half of the nose, then add a slightly curved gleam across the upper half. Make a very narrow line just above and parallel to the chin to suggest the gleam of a lower lip there. Rinse your brush well, then add small dots of light in the upper half of the eyes.

17 Finish the backside.

Switch to a larger stiff, flat brush, preferably one that's become slightly ragged with wear. You may want to experiment with a grass comb here. Mix black and white to make a medium to light shade of gray. Add enough water to allow the paint to flow smoothly, then apply clusters of strokes to the black fur along the back, following the diagram provided on page 247. Use slanted rows of strokes along either side of the spine to indicate that the fur divides along that line, then work out and down, leaving dark spaces between sets of soft gleams as well as between other features such as the rounded tops of the haunches and the area along the lighter mane on both sides.

Go back with a much lighter gray and a script liner and add a row of lighter, more delicate fur lines to the upper center of each gleam to suggest more glossiness.

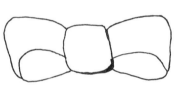

18 **Add a bow.**
Your bow can be any color you choose. I used Sunshine Yellow. Place the bow so that it nearly spans the space between the ears about halfway up. Fill in the bow shape with your base color. Darken your bow color with a touch of black and use this to outline the center knot and to indicate shadows below the top of the bow loops. Highlight the top edges of the loops and the top of the knot by adding a bit of white to the original color.

Seal your Yorkie and enjoy his winsome company for life.

How to Paint a Yorkie

More Ideas

Lap Dogs

This rock was nearly perfect for a Yorkie pup—I just built up the ears a bit with wood putty.

Pomeranians and Maltese are two more lap type dogs that seem made to order for rock painting.

This perky Scottie needed an unusual rock to accommodate his ears.

Poodle fur can be a challenge. Try applying it with a deerfoot stippler over a contrasting basecoat. For definition, add a small twist to each dabbing stroke.

Short-Haired Dogs

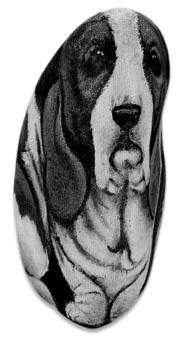

Can you see how
the proportions dif-
fer between a pup
and a full grown
Labrador?

Puppies grow up
too quickly, so a
rock pup like this
Lab makes a won-
derful souvenir of
your dog's puppy-
hood.

This rock practically begged me to turn it
into a mournful Basset Hound.

Here's a napping Beagle.

Choose elongated rocks for dachshunds.

Long-Haired Dogs

Golden retrievers, collies, schnauzers and
cocker spaniels are more examples of long-
haired dogs.

Try painting a whole basketful of fluffy pups.

This "pocket pet" sized portrait of a
German shepherd would make a great
paperweight.

Other Ideas

Here's a portrait of a wire-haired terrier.

Whether or not they get along in real life, you can always paint a loving family portrait of your pets.

You couldn't help but take these little orphans if left on your doorstep.

Painting on

Rocks

for Kids

NORTH LIGHT BOOKS
CINCINNATI, OHIO
www.artistsnetwork.com

Lin Wellford

here are the projects
you can do!

tips for painting rocks

Rocks are a great natural art material. They come in many different shapes and sizes. By adding details with paint, you can turn rocks into all kinds of amazing things. Pick up a rock and ask yourself what it looks like.

Not all rocks are good for painting. Some are too bumpy or rough, or they soak up paint like a sponge. Look for rocks that are smooth. Rocks that have been tumbled in water, such as in a river or creek, are the easiest to paint, but you can also use chunky rocks and pieces of fieldstone as long as the sides are not too rough. You can even paint pieces of broken concrete.

➲ Always scrub your rocks before you begin painting. Paint won't stick to a dirty rock.

➲ You'll need a paper plate, plastic lid or plastic artist's palette for mixing your paint.

➲ Never let paint dry on your brushes. It turns them all stiff and yucky.

A clean paintbrush

is a happy paintbrush.

➲ Always rinse your brush between colors. Have paper towels handy for wiping your brush.

➲ Pour paint in little puddles, about the size of your thumbnail. Big puddles dry up before you can use them.

➲ Wear old clothes and push up your sleeves when you paint. If you get acrylic paint on your clothes, scrub it off with an old toothbrush, soap and plenty of water before it dries. Dried acrylic paint may never come out of fabric.

➲ Spread newspaper over your work area. You can wipe your brush and make test strokes on it. Also it will slow down a spill if you tip over your water.

And the most important thing to remember is

➲ You can't ruin a rock! If you make a mistake, just wipe off the paint before it dries, or let it dry and then paint over it.

Remember to rinse your brush

after each color.

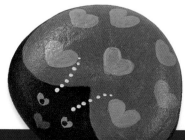

Paint

tempera paint

For the projects in this book, you'll need a set of basic colors of acrylic paint. You can also decorate rocks with tempera paint, watercolors, paint pens, markers, gel pens, colored pencils or nail polish.

acrylic paint

If your painted rocks will be just for decoration indoors, the kind of paint you use doesn't matter. If your rocks are going to be used outside or soaked in water, you should use outdoor acrylic paint, which is found at most craft stores. It stays on the rocks better than regular acrylic paint.

outdoor acrylic paint

Paintbrushes

You will need just three brushes:
- a wide flat brush like the two brushes on the far right
- a medium brush like the two in the middle
- a small, skinny brush like the green one

Other helpful things
- Cotton swabs for blending
- Pencil, marker or white pencil for drawing the designs on the rocks
- Air-dry clay for rocks that tip over
- Dimensional paint for puffy lines or dots
- Acrylic floor wax for making the rocks shiny

brushes, paint and more

colored pencils

263

all about rocks

Where to find rocks

You may find good rocks near creeks, streams, beaches and lakes. In some areas rocks seem to be lying around every-where, and in other places it may take a lot of hunting to find them. Don't take rocks out of the water in places where they may be homes for crayfish or other animals. State and national parks do not allow visitors to take any-thing home, including rocks. It's a good idea to ask for permission before you gather rocks outside your own yard.

You can buy rocks of all sizes from landscaping companies or gardening stores. Once you start looking for rocks, you'll be amazed at the unexpected places you'll find them.

Small rocks are fun, too!

Most of the rocks in this book fit into the palm of your hand. If you can't find many rocks this size, don't worry; there are still lots of things you can do with smaller rocks. Here are just a few ideas.

Make Faces
Use flat pebbles to create silly face rocks.

Put 'em Together
Use white glue and pebbles or gravel to make pictures, names or designs. Colored aquarium gravel is sold at pet stores. Make sure to allow plenty of drying time when you glue rocks.

Message Rocks
Do you have something to say? Write it on stone!

Name Game
Amaze your friends with special rocks painted just for them! These make great party favors, too.

Clever Constructions
Even the tiniest pebbles can be glued together with white glue to create all kinds of fun stuff. Use crumpled foil to hold the pebbles in place while the glue dries. Wait until the next day to start painting them.

265

PROJECT 1

go fish!

66 I wanted a pet fish, but Mom said I had to wait until I was old enough to remember to feed it. At the creek I saw a rock that gave me an idea. Why not make a rock fish? A rock fish doesn't mind if I never feed him! Here's how I made mine. 99

Make a Fishbowl

Put gravel or marbles in the bottom of a fishbowl and add water, a plastic plant and your painted fish (painted with outdoor acrylic paint). Prop up your fish with a smaller rock. Paint other rocks to add to the scene.

What You'll Need

- Rock
- Pencil
- Palette or paper plate
- Paint of your choice*
- Paintbrushes
- Black marker (optional)
- Glitter paint or white glue and glitter** (optional)

*If you aren't planning to put your fish in a bowl of water, you can use any kind of paint. If you are, use outdoor acrylic paint.
**White glue and glitter isn't waterproof.

1

Find a fish-shaped rock

Choose a smooth, flat rock that has a "fishy" shape. Pictures of real fish can give you ideas. When you find a rock you like, scrub it clean.

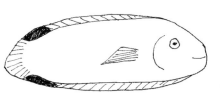

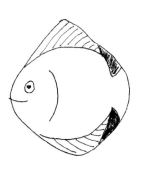

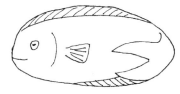

2

Draw the fish

Use a pencil to draw the head with a curved line and give the fish a round eye. At the other end, draw a fan-shaped tail and draw triangles above and below the tail.

You can use these fish as guides for drawing your fish. Or you can enlarge them on a copier and trace one onto your rock with carbon paper.

3

Paint the head

Use a bright color and your large brush to paint the fish's head. Paint all the way around the edges so no plain rock shows, but leave the circle for the eye unpainted.

4

Paint around the tail

Use black paint and your medium brush to fill in the triangles above and below the tail. The black paint makes those parts seem to disappear.

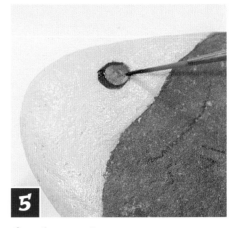

5

Outline the eye

Make a black outline around the eye with a black marker or your skinny brush, keeping the outside edge round and neat. The inside edge will get covered up later.

Remember to rinse your brush

after each color.

6

Paint the body

Pick a color for the body. Mix three drops of this color with one drop of white, and paint the fish's body.

7

Paint the tail

Mix three drops of white and one drop of the body color for the tail. Save this puddle of paint for step 9.

TIPS FOR PAINTING GOOD LINES

1. Thin the paint with a little water.
2. Hold your brush handle straight up.
3. Paint with just the tip of the brush.
4. Paint lines with one smooth stroke, not a lot of little sketchy lines.
5. If you mess up, wipe the line off with a damp paper towel and try again.
6. The more you practice, the better you'll get!

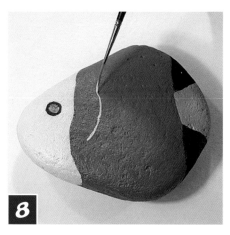

Paint the gill

When the paint on the body is dry, use your skinny brush to add a light-colored curved gill line just behind the head. I used yellow.

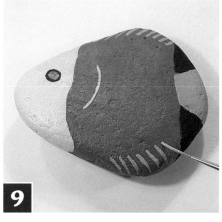

Paint fins

Clean the skinny brush, and dip it in the tail color to paint short, slanted lines for the top and bottom fins.

Paint the eye and lip

Use your skinny brush with red paint to fill in the middle of the eye. Then make a red line for the mouth. Rinse the brush, and use black paint to paint a pupil in the eye.

Add white lines

Use your skinny brush to make a small fan-shaped fin behind and below the gill line. Also add some lines to the tail, curving them out at the top and bottom to fit the fin shape.

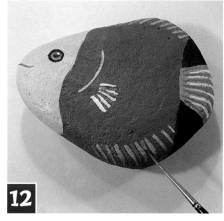

Dot the eye

Last, add a tiny dot of white off center in your fish's eye. For extra decoration, I painted little purple lines between all the fin and tail lines.

Add finishing touches

If you want, you can paint your fish with glitter paint or (if you won't be putting your fish in water) white glue sprinkled with glitter. I also added dots of paint to the body.

269

rocky roadsters

66 I made a race-track in my sandbox and I needed some cars to put on the roads. My brother said sand would jam up the wheels of toy cars, so I decided to make "rockmobiles" instead. This is how I made them. 99

Rock

Pencil

Palette or paper plate

Paint of your choice

Paintbrushes

Black marker (optional)

Acrylic floor wax (optional)

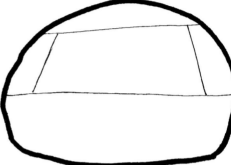

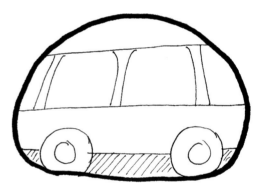

1

Pick a car-shaped rock

Rocks with flat bottoms and rounded tops make good cars. Rocks with square corners can be trucks. You might even find a rock shaped like a roadster with a long hood. Wash your rock and scrub away any slimy stuff.

2

Draw the car

Follow the steps above to draw a car on your rock. Use a pencil so you can erase any mistakes.

Here's how I drew the car on my rock.

3

Paint the tires

Mix two drops of white with one drop of black to make gray. Use your small brush to fill in all the wheel circles. All four wheels should be the same size and as round as you can make them.

Remember to rinse your brush

after each color.

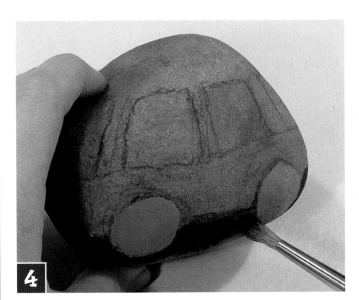

4

Make part of the rock "disappear"

It's almost magical the way painting an area black makes that part of the rock seem to vanish. Use black paint to fill in the space around the bottoms of the wheels and below the car body on both sides and each end.

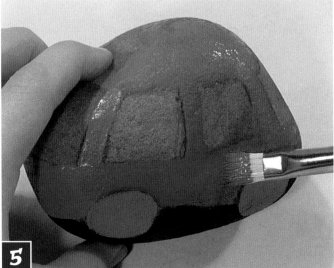

5

Paint the car body

Pick a color for your car. Dark colors cover in one coat, but a light color may need two coats. Use your medium brush to paint the sides and ends. Then paint the top. Let the paint dry before going to the next step.

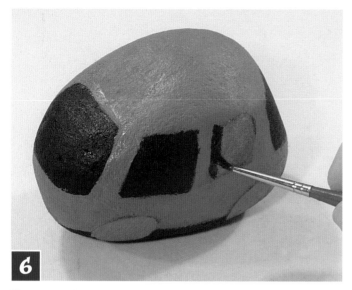

Paint the windows

Paint the windows black. Use the skinny brush to paint around the edges, making them as smooth and straight as you can. Then use a bigger brush to fill in the centers.

Paint the wheel hubs

While you still have black paint on your skinny brush, make a big circle in the center of each wheel and fill it in with solid black. Make all these wheel hubs the same size.

Paint the fenders

Use a black marker or your skinny brush with black paint thinned with a little water to paint the curved fenders above each wheel. Connect the front and back fenders with a straight line. Paint two lines for the door (see step 10 for a picture of the door).

Paint the bumpers

Clean your brush. Between the fenders, use white to paint bumpers with rounded corners. Paint a license plate on the back bumper. After the paint dries, use the skinny brush or a marker to paint letters or numbers on the license plate.

10

Paint wheel spokes

Use your skinny brush to paint a white circle inside each black hub circle. Paint an X in the middle, then paint a line sideways and one up and down.

11

Paint the door handles

Then use the same brush to paint white curved lines for the door handles.

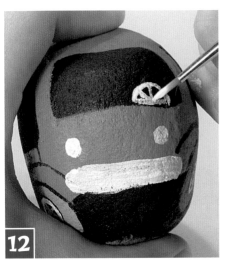

12

Paint the steering wheel

Use the same brush to paint a white steering wheel on the driver's side of the front windshield. Paint round white headlights and smaller taillights. Painting white first will make the red and yellow paint show up better.

13

Paint headlights and taillights

When the white is dry, use red paint for the taillights and bright yellow paint for the headlights. You can add sparkle with glitter paint if you want. For a shiny car, paint it with clear acrylic floor wax.

more ideas

rocky roadsters

SCHOOL BUS

③ lazy lizards

> A big green lizard was sunning himself on a rock in our garden. When I tried to catch him, he scurried away, so I took the rock inside and painted my own lizard on it. This lizard never runs away from me! Here is how I did it.

What You'll Need

Large rock

Pencil

Palette or paper plate

Paint of your choice

Paintbrushes

Dimensional paint (optional)

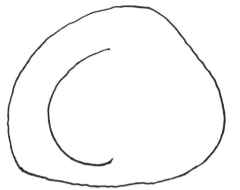

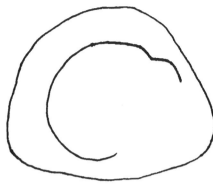

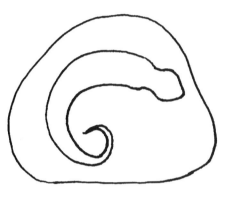

Follow these steps to draw a lizard

1

Choose a rock and draw the lizard

Your rock should be smooth and have enough room in the middle to fit a lizard's curved body and tail. Scrub the rock and draw the lizard on it. Trace this lizard and enlarge it on a copy machine or draw your own lizard following the steps shown above.

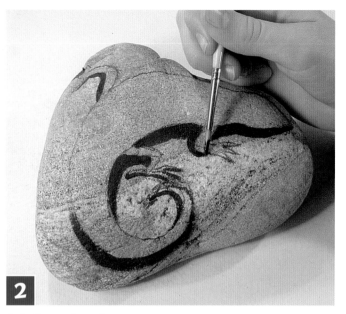

2
Make shadows

Use black paint and your small brush to paint thick black shadows around part of the lizard. Make the shadows below the legs thinner.

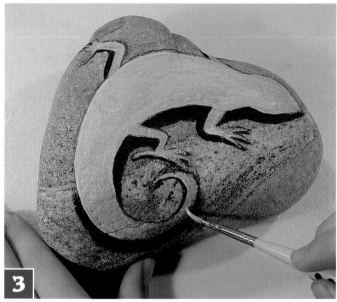

3
Paint the lizard yellow

Rinse your brush and paint the lizard yellow to make the final coat of paint look brighter. Use a small brush to outline the lizard and to fill in the toes and the tip of the tail. Then use a bigger brush to fill in the rest.

4
Paint the body

I painted my lizard green, but yours can be any color you like. Use your medium brush to paint the top of the lizard's body, leaving an oval-shaped area for the eye. Also leave his tummy and parts of the tail and legs yellow. Use your skinny brush for the toes, tip of the tail and under the eye.

5
Add stripes

Mix a darker color (I mixed blue and green). Use your small brush to paint a line along the top edge of the yellow tummy, the legs, tail and top of the body.

PAINTING TIP

A long line should be painted in one long, smooth stroke instead of lots of small sketchy lines.

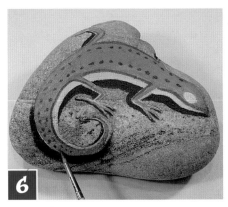

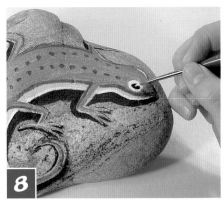

Add rows of spots

Use the same color to make two rows of dots from the neck to the end of the tail, making the dots smaller as you go. Make them big enough so you can paint yellow spots on top.

Fill in the eye

Rinse your brush and use black paint to paint a small oval eye in the center of the yellow eye area. Give the eye pointed ends like a little football. Also make two tiny black dots for nostrils at the end of the nose.

Paint white highlights

Use your small brush to add a line of white along the bottom edge of the lizard to help the yellow tummy stand out. Paint white on the neck, under the chin and around the eye. Make a tiny white dot in the eye.

Add finishing touches

Use a small brush or dimensional paint to paint a yellow dot on the top edge of each blue-green spot so that a little of the darker color shows.

Lizards and salamanders can be painted in a rainbow of colors. Paint a whole collection to decorate your rock garden or fill a terrarium.

4
flower power

66 My grand-mother's birthday was coming, and I wanted to make something special for her. She really likes flowers, so I thought; "Why not paint a flower rock for her?" She loves it! Here's how I did it. 99

What You'll Need

- Large rock
- Pencil
- White colored pencil
- Palette or paper plate
- Paint of your choice
- Paintbrushes
- Clear acrylic spray (optional)

1

Choose a rock

Lots of rock sizes and shapes make good flower rocks. You can use round rocks or chunky rocks that will stand up on one flat end. Whatever the shape, rocks that have mostly smooth surfaces are the easiest to paint. When you have your rock, scrub it and let it dry.

2

Divide your rock

Use a pencil to make a line around the bottom third of your rock. Keep this line as level as possible all the way around or your flower bowl will look uneven.

Remember to rinse your brush

after each color.

3

Paint the bowl

Pick a color for the bowl. I chose blue to match my grandmother's sofa. Add two drops of white to this color. Use your biggest brush to paint the bowl all the way down to the bottom. Let the paint dry.

Paint the background

Rinse your brush and mix green with enough black to make a very dark green. A dark color behind the leaves and flowers will make them stand out. Paint this color from the top down to the bowl. Let the paint dry.

Draw the leaves

Use a white pencil to draw different-size oval leaves. Start with a cluster at the top, then work down. Overlap the leaves and draw a few that hang over the edge of the bowl. It's OK to have irregular spaces between the leaves.

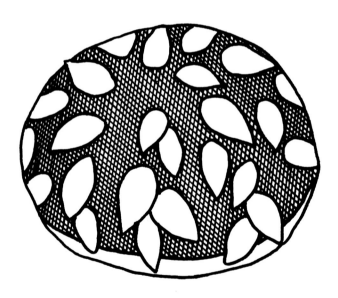

Your leaves should look something like this.

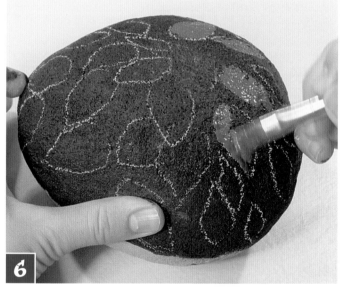

Paint some of the leaves

Use a small or medium brush and green paint to paint all the leaves at the very top of your rock. Then use this same color to paint other leaves here and there.

7

Paint light green leaves

Rinse your brush and mix equal amounts of yellow and green to make light green. Use this to paint more leaves, again skipping around.

8

Paint the rest of the leaves

Finally, add a little more green to the light green mixture to make an in-between color and paint the rest of the leaves.

9

Detail the leaves

Mix a little black with green to make dark green. Use a skinny brush to add a crease down the center of all the dark green leaves. Use plain green to paint the creases in the other leaves. Use black paint to outline the places where the leaves overlap.

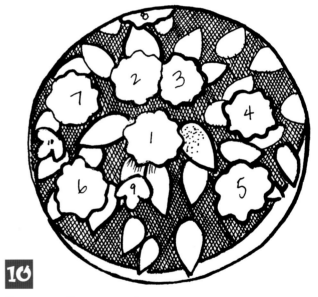

10

Draw flower shapes

When the paint is dry, use a white pencil to draw three flowers in the center (numbers 1, 2 and 3 above). Add others around the edges (4 to 8). Numbers 9 and 10 are buds. Draw some flowers close together and others farther apart.

11

Paint white flowers

Use your medium brush and white paint to fill in all the flower shapes. Let it dry and paint a second coat if needed.

12

Add petal details

An easy way to paint flowers is to paint a curl in the middle of each flower with a small brush and red paint. Begin in the center each time. The spirals will look better if they are a little uneven or if there are small gaps in the lines.

13

Add flower buds

Fill in any plain-looking places with a few flower buds. Mix pale pink by adding a touch of red to a drop of white. Use your medium brush to make a center oval shape and add two smaller ovals, one on each side.

14

Paint bud details

Use your small brush with red paint to outline the inside edges of the two side ovals, and one straight line up the center. Rinse the brush and use the dark green from step 9 to paint a cluster of lines on the top of the bud.

more ideas

flower power

There are lots of ways to paint flowers on rocks.

If you want to make your rock shiny, ask an adult to please spray it with clear acrylic spray, which also protects the paint. If you used outdoor acrylic paint, your flower rocks can be displayed outside.

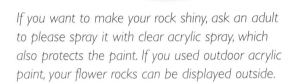

You can paint flowers on a rock that is too uneven to stand on its own. "Plant" it in a flowerpot!

rockosaurs

66 What would it be like to have a dinosaur for a pet? I guess I'd need a bigger room! I painted some dinosaurs on rocks and took them to school when we were studying prehistoric reptiles. Everyone thought they were cool. 99

What You'll Need ↴

Large rock

Pencil

Palette or paper plate

Paint of your choice

Paintbrushes

Cotton swab (optional)

Black marker (optional)

2

Paint a basecoat

A coat of yellow paint will make the final paint color look brighter, especially on dark-colored rocks. Use your large brush to paint the whole rock, except for the very bottom. Let the paint dry before you go on. Clean your brush.

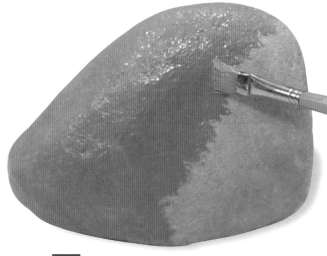

1

Choose a rock

Rocks with flat bottoms and curving tops work best. Scrub your rock clean. If the bottom of your rock is not level, add air-dry clay to the wet rock as shown on page 301. Let the clay dry overnight before painting your rock.

3

Paint the rock orange

Paint the rock orange, which is red mixed with yellow, or choose another color. Let it dry.

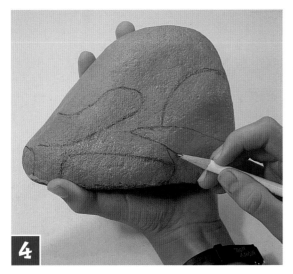

Draw the dinosaur

Follow the drawings to draw a dinosaur on your rock.

On the front of your rock, draw an oval about the size of your thumbprint. Add neck lines to the head, curving them down and around the corner of the rock but leaving room below the bottom neck line for the front legs.

Draw the tail so the tip points to the neck. Draw the front leg, then a tummy line from behind the front leg to the tail.

Make a big oval haunch that curves above the top of the tail. Draw a back foot where the tail curves up from the bottom of the rock.

Turn your rock around and draw the other front leg. Draw another oval haunch and back leg plus a tummy line between the two legs.

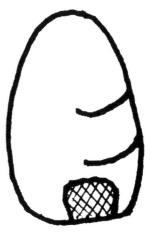

Here is the way your rock should look from the front edge.

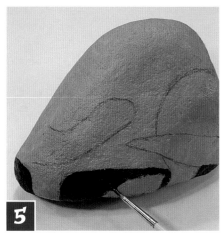

5

Paint the open spaces

Use a medium or large brush with black paint to darken the spaces around the legs and below the body.

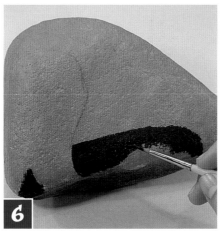

6

Paint black on the back

Also darken the spaces between the two front legs and around the legs on the back of the rock.

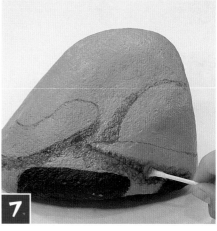

7

Add shading

Add enough water to some brown paint so you can see through it. Use a cotton swab or paintbrush to add brown shadows below the head and neck, around the haunch and under the tail. Before the paint dries, soften the edges of the shadows by rubbing them with a dry paintbrush.

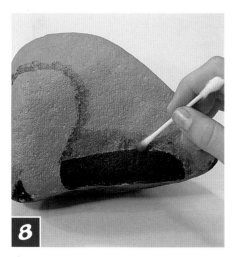

8

Add shading to the back

Add shadows to the back of your dinosaur around the haunch and on the bottom of the tummy.

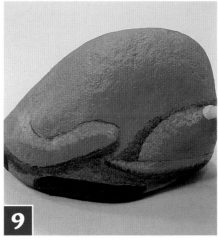

9

Paint highlights

Mix two drops of yellow with one drop of white. Use a damp cotton swab or medium stiff brush to scrub this color along the top half of the head and neck, the top of the haunch and the top of the tail. Soften the edges with a dry paintbrush.

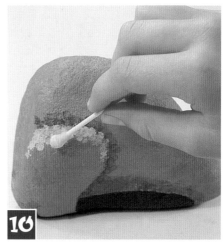

10

Repeat

Paint highlights along the top edge of the haunch on the back side, too.

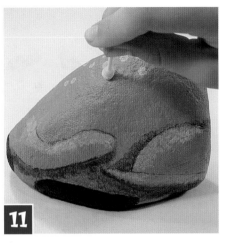

11

Add spots

Use the same cotton swab (or a small brush) and yellow paint to add clusters of spots to the top of the dinosaur.

12

Add black details

Use your small brush and black paint (or a black marker) to make a tiny dot for a nostril, a curved mouth line and a round eye. Then outline the head, neck, haunches and tail with black paint to make them stand out.

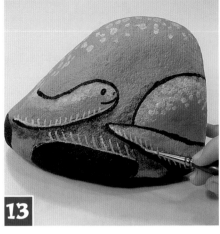

13

Add yellow details

Rinse your brush and make light outlines along the tummy, the tail and the neck with the yellow paint from step 9. Add a row of short, curved lines to the bottom edge of the tail and longer curved lines on the tummy. Turn the rock over and paint tummy lines on the back of the dinosaur.

14

Add white touches

Use your small brush and white paint to make a tiny C shape inside the black eye circle. If you mess up, let the paint dry, then fix it with black paint. Paint a white dot in the eye. Add three half-circle toenails to each foot.

15

Create more texture

Pick up a little red paint with a clean, damp cotton swab or your small brush to add more dots to the dinosaur's back and the tops of the haunches. Add smaller dots to the yellow places on the neck and tail.

Look at your rock from every angle to make sure it looks finished.

There are lots of other kinds of dinosaurs that you can paint on rocks. You could even try turning a dinosaur into a dragon!

go buggy!

" When I told my friends I was going to give them cooties, you should have seen the faces they made! Now everyone wants me to "bug" them! Here is how I painted my cootie bugs. "

What You'll Need

Rock

White colored pencil

Palette or paper plate

Paint of your choice

Paintbrushes

Black marker (optional)

Glitter paint (optional)

1 # Pick a rock

Any size smooth, round or oval rock will work, but tiny rocks may be harder to paint. Scrub it clean.

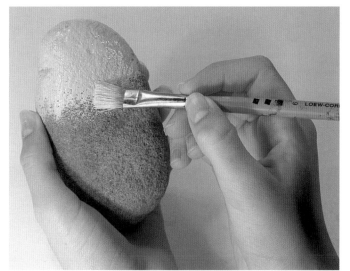

2

Paint a basecoat

Use a big flat brush to paint the top and sides of your rock with a light color of paint. You can leave the bottom unpainted. Let the paint dry.

3

Sketch the design

Use a white pencil to draw the bug. Make a line for the head, and add three curved lines for stripes. You may use a regular pencil, but draw the lines lightly so they won't show through the paint.

293

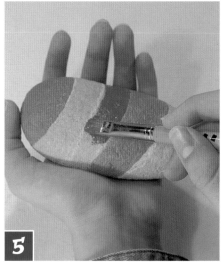

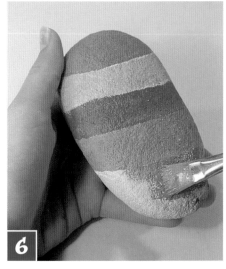

Paint the head and one stripe

Pick a different color and use your large brush to paint the head, making the edges neat and round. Then paint the third stripe this color.

Paint another stripe

Rinse your brush. When the paint is dry, paint the second stripe with bright red or a different color of your choice.

Paint the last stripe

Rinse your brush, then choose another color to paint the back end of the bug, covering the basecoat to the very bottom edges of the rock. I used a mixture of yellow and green.

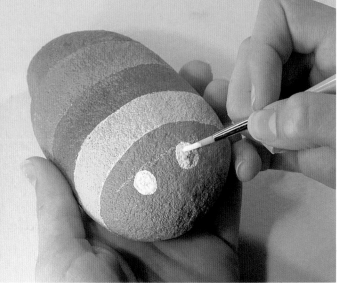

Draw and paint the eyes

To keep the eyes level, sketch a straight line across the top part of the head and draw two round eyes that are the same size. Use your small brush and white paint to fill in the eye circles.

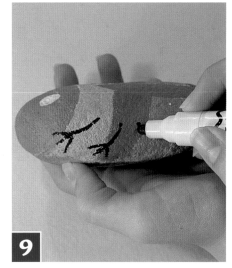

Draw and paint the wings

When the stripes are dry, draw two long oval wings that come to points at the center of the first stripe. Use a large or medium brush and a new color of paint to fill in these wing shapes. I used purple.

Add legs and feet

Use your small brush and black paint (or a black marker) to draw three curved legs on each side of its body. Draw the feet any shape you wish.

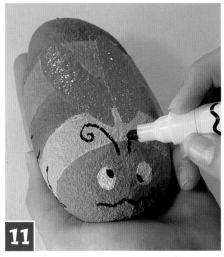

Remember to rinse your brush

after each color.

Add glitter if you want

I added glitter paint to the wings, but you may want to put glitter on one of the stripes instead. Use your imagination to make your bug special.

Add details

Use a black marker or a small brush and black paint to give your bug a wiggly mouth line, two goofy-looking eyeballs and a pair of curly feelers.

more ideas

There are lots of different bugs you can paint, from ones that look real to some that are really silly.

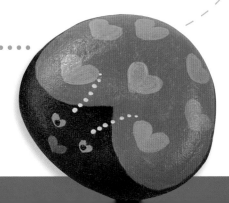

295

sandbox city

" My rock cars gave me the idea to make a city to go with them. I looked around and found lots of rocks shaped like all kinds of buildings. They were fun to paint, too. Here's how you can make a really easy rock house. "

Rock

Pencil

Palette or paper plate

Paint of your choice

Paintbrushes

Cotton swab (optional)

Black marker (optional)

1

Pick a rock

Rocks for buildings should have flat bottoms and flat fronts. Rocks with square tops make good stores. Houses should have slanted or pointed tops. Scrub the rock clean.

2

Draw the design

Use a pencil to sketch the door in the center of the rock. Draw square or rectangular windows on each side of the door so that the tops line up. Make a third window near the top. Draw two straight lines along the front, sides and the back for the roof. If your rock is thick enough, add windows to the sides of the rock.

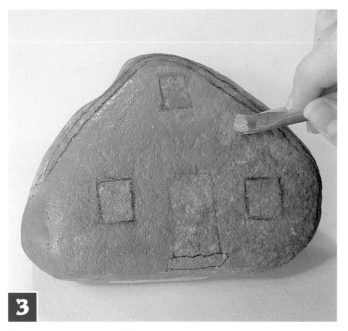

3

Paint the walls

Your house may be any color you like. I mixed black and white to make gray. Use a large or medium brush to paint the front, sides and back of your house, leaving the doors, windows and roof unpainted.

4

Paint the roof

Rinse your brush and paint the roof but not the area under it, which is called the eaves. I painted my roof black. Other good color combinations are white walls with a dark green roof, light blue walls with a navy blue roof, yellow walls with a brown roof, and red walls with a white roof.

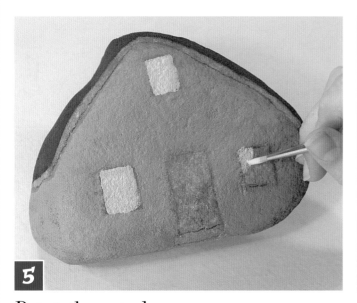

5

Paint the windows

Yellow windows make your house look cheerful and cozy. If your walls are yellow, paint the windows orange or a dark color. Use your small brush, and make the edges of the windows as straight as you can.

6

Add a glow

Mix a tiny amount of orange (red plus yellow). Use the tip of your finger, a damp cotton swab or a small, dry brush to rub this color on the bottom part of each window.

Paint the door and eaves

Use a small or medium brush and white paint to neatly fill in the shape of the door, keeping the edges smooth and straight. If there is room, add a doorstep below the door. Paint a white line under the roof for the eaves.

Add black outlines

Use black paint and the skinny brush or a black marker to outline the door, the doorstep and the windows. Make a cross in each window. Straight lines in the corners help make the house look square. Add a doorknob.

Paint some bushes

Rinse your brush and mix green with a small amount of black to make dark green. Use this paint and your small brush to make pointed oval bushes on each side of the door and at the two corners of the house.

Paint flowers

Rinse your brush and switch to plain green to paint flower stems under each window. Keep them shorter than the bushes. Let these lines dry and rinse your brush before adding red flowers to the tops and middles of the stems.

Paint flowers on the bushes

Use the very tip of your skinniest brush to add dots for tiny flowers all over the bushes. I used purple. Now your rock house is finished!

11

more ideas

TOY STORE

GAS STATION

There are lots of other kinds of rock buildings you can paint to add to your sandbox city. Look at the buildings in your neighborhood for ideas.

SWEET SHOP

how to fix
a wobbly rock!

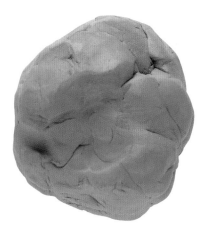

What do you do with a rock that won't stand up? Add some air-dry clay to the bottom. The place where the clay was added won't show once the rock has been painted. This air-dry clay is sold at craft stores, but you can use any kind of clay that hardens without baking.

1

Scrub the rock clean. Clay sticks best to a wet rock.

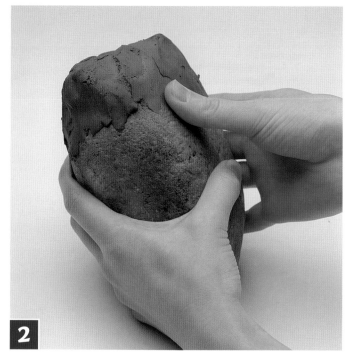

2

Put clay on the bottom of the rock and smooth it with your fingers. There shouldn't be any bumps where the clay and the rock meet.

3

Stand the rock on a table so the bottom of the clay becomes flat. If the rock still tips over, add more clay until the rock stands up. Leave the rock alone for 24 hours until the clay is dry.

301

playful food

66 Did you ever pretend to run a restaurant? You can paint rocks to look like lots of different kinds of food. I made hamburgers for my picnic table restaurant. My dad thought they looked so good that he bought one to use as a paperweight on his desk. Here's how I made them. 99

What You'll Need

- Rock
- Pencil
- White colored pencil
- Palette or paper plate
- Paint of your choice
- Paintbrushes
- White dimensional paint (optional)

2

Draw the bun lines

Draw a line all around the rock, a little bit above the center. Make another line below the first line, leaving enough space for the burger patty and toppings.

1

Find a hamburger-shaped rock

Look for round rocks that are flat on the bottom and rounded on top. They can be as big or small as you wish, but a rock that fits into your hand is perfect. Scrub the rock clean and let it dry.

3

Paint the meat

Use your large or medium brush and brown paint to paint the meat, keeping the top and bottom edges as smooth and level as you can. Let the paint dry.

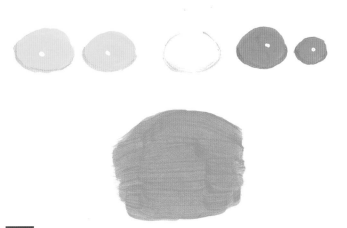

4

Mix paint for the bun

Use your large brush to mix two drops of yellow, one drop of white, and one and a half drops of orange. Put a small drop of brown on your palette and pick up a little on the tip of your brush. Add it to the mix. Add touches of brown and white until the mixture is the color of a bun.

5

Paint the bun

Use your large brush to cover the entire top half of the bun with the bun color. When you are finished, don't rinse your brush, but use it to mix the next color.

6

Paint a tan ring and the bottom bun

The bun should be lighter just above the meat. Mix a drop or two of white paint with the paint left on your brush to make tan. Paint a narrow ring just above the meat. Use a dry brush to soften the edge where the two colors meet. Paint the bottom bun this tan color, too.

Prop up your rock with a brush or a pencil when you paint the bottom bun. Let the paint dry before going on.

Remember to rinse your brush

after each color.

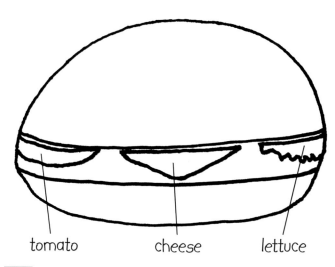

tomato   cheese   lettuce

7

Add the fillings

Use a white pencil to sketch four cheese triangles equally spaced around your meat. In the upper half of the meat, sketch a half-round tomato slice between the first two triangles, a ruffled edge of lettuce leaf between the next two, then another tomato slice and a final lettuce leaf.

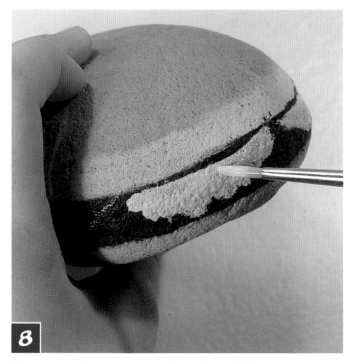

8

Paint a basecoat for the fillings

To help the fillings stand out, use your medium brush with yellow to paint all the shapes you just sketched. Leave a narrow ring of brown paint showing along the tops of the fillings. Make sure the edge of the lettuce looks wavy.

9

Paint the cheese and tomato

Rinse your brush. Then mix a tiny amount of red into a small drop of yellow to make a cheese color. Paint all four cheese triangles with this color. Rinse your brush and use red paint to paint the two tomato slices.

Paint the lettuce

Rinse your brush. Squeeze out a drop of yellow paint and add a little white and green to make a pale green color. Paint the two lettuce leaves, leaving a line of brown just above them.

Detail the lettuce

Add more green to the lettuce color and use this darker shade to paint short lines on the lettuce so it looks ruffled.

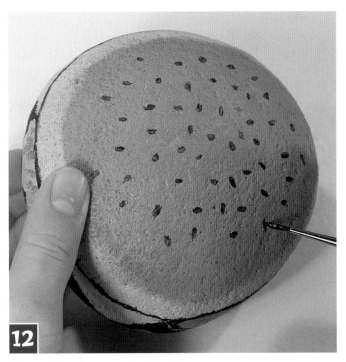

Dot the top of the bun

Use your smallest brush and brown paint to paint small dark dots over the top of the bun. (I made about fifty!) Don't put any around the sides.

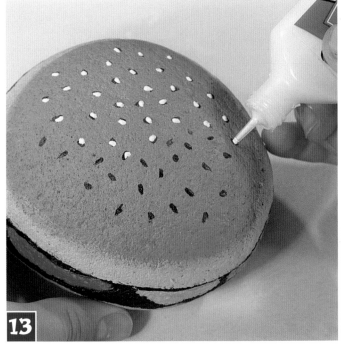

Add sesame seeds

You can paint the seeds with white paint, or you can make real-looking seeds with white dimensional paint. Touch the tip of the bottle just off center of each brown spot, then lift up sideways. A rim of brown should show on one side. If you mess up, use a damp cotton swab to pick up the paint. When all the seeds are painted, let it dry for an hour.

more ideas

playful food

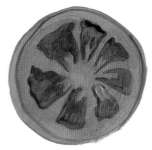

Try painting some pickle chips and sliced tomatoes to serve with your "burgers."

If you use your imagination when looking for food-shaped rocks, there is no telling what you'll find: sandwiches, cookies, fruit, or slices of pie or pizza, to name just a few!

PROJECT

9

mystery
eggs

66 What if you discovered a strange-looking
egg just as it was starting to hatch? What
kind of creature would be inside? A dragon?
A dinosaur? An alien? Maybe even a monster?
Paint one and maybe you'll find out! 99

Large rock

Pencil

White colored pencil (optional)

Palette or paper plate

Paint of your choice

Paintbrushes

Sponge

Silver acrylic paint (optional)

Glow-in-the-dark paint (optional)

Black marker (optional)

1

Choose an egg-shaped rock

Any of these rocks would make a good egg. Look for an oval rock that is shaped like an egg. It can be any size, but one that is about as big as your fist makes a good first egg. Scrub it clean and let it dry.

2

Paint the basecoat

Use your large brush to mix two big drops of white with one big drop of black. Paint your entire rock with this gray color. Let it dry before going to the next step.

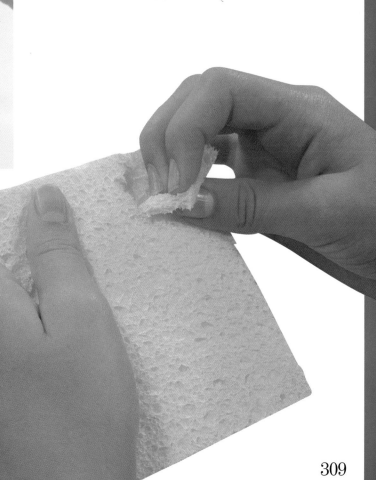

3

Tear a sponge

Tear a small piece from a kitchen sponge so that it has ragged edges. Wet it and squeeze most of the water out.

Sponge on purple paint

Use a brush to spread a small puddle of purple paint (red mixed with blue) on your palette. Lightly press the damp sponge piece into the paint. Dab the sponge on a piece of newspaper, then pat it on your painted rock, turning it in different directions. You may have to do this several times. Let the paint dry.

Sponge on blue paint

Pour out a small puddle of blue paint. Rinse your sponge and squeeze it almost dry. Sponge blue paint on your rock just as you did in step 4. Let the paint dry. Rinse your sponge clean.

Sponge on silver paint

Now sponge on a coat of silver acrylic paint. If you don't have silver paint, use light gray. Sponge this color lightly so that the other colors show through. Let the paint dry.

7 Outline the opening

Sketch a diamond-shaped opening on your rock, using the drawing at left as a guide. Use your small brush and black paint to outline the shape of the jagged hole. Wiggle your brush as you paint to make wavy lines.

8

Paint the center

Switch to your large brush to fill in the center of the shape with solid black.

9

Create large cracks

Use your smallest brush and black paint to paint large cracks around the outside of the opening. Make some thick and some thin, some short and some longer so that they don't look too much alike.

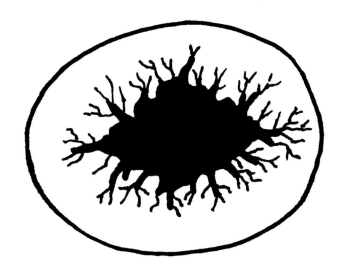

Remember
to rinse
your brush

after
each color.

10

Make tiny cracks

To make the smaller cracks, you can use a fine-tip black marker or a paint pen. Or mix a little water with some black paint and use the tip of your small brush to paint thin crooked lines that fan out from the ends of the cracks, some with two lines, some with more.

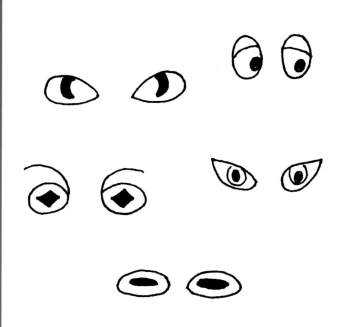

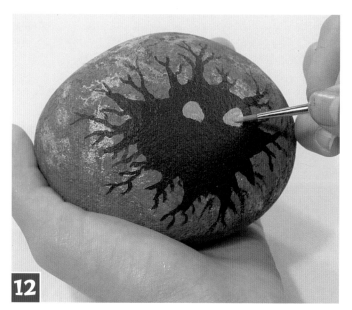

11

Paint the eyes

When the black paint is dry, use your small brush and white paint to paint two small eyes that are the same size. The eyes can be any shape you like. It may help to sketch them first with a white pencil. Let the paint dry.

12

Paint the eye color

Mix lime green from yellow with just a touch of blue, or use glow-in-the-dark paint for a spooky effect. Use your small brush to paint this color over the white eye shapes.

13

Paint the pupils

Clean your small brush, then use black paint or a black marker to add two pupils. I made mine narrow and curved like cats' eyes. The pupils you paint may be different.

more ideas

mystery eggs

Eggs can be painted in lots of different color combinations. Try adding the hint of a face with a long, forked tongue, or a scaly tail slipping out and perhaps a little claw showing, too.

bookend bears

" Everyone in my family is crazy about teddy bears! I found an easy way to paint them on rocks. They make great bookends, but you can also use them as doorstops, paperweights or decorations for your room. "

What You'll Need 🐦

Large rock

Pencil

Palette or paper plate

Paint of your choice

Paintbrushes

Cotton swab (optional)

Marker (optional)

1

Find a bear-shaped rock

Look for tall rocks with flat bottoms. They can have a slight tilt to them. Medium-size ones are easiest to paint. Scrub the rock clean. If your rock won't stand up, add air-dry clay to the bottom as shown on page 301. Let the clay dry overnight before painting your rock.

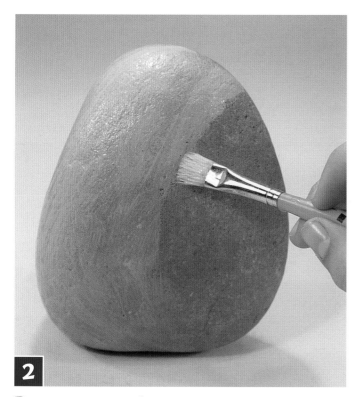

2

Paint your rock

Use your large brush to paint the entire rock the color you've chosen for your bear. If your rock is dark, you may need to add a second coat. Let the paint dry.

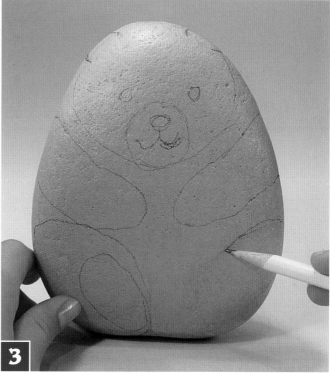

3

Sketch the bear

Use a pencil to draw the bear on your rock, following the drawings on the next page.

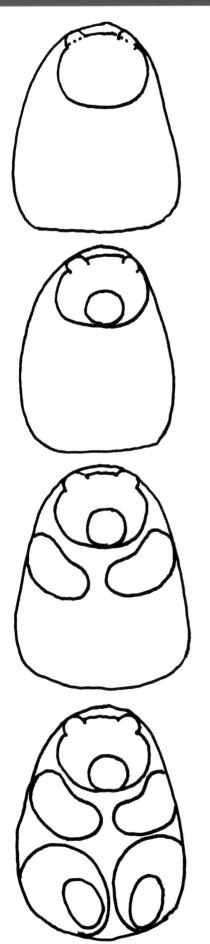

Follow the drawings to sketch your bear.

4

Paint dark outlines

Use dark paint and a small brush or a marker to paint over the pencil lines. Use brown paint if your bear is yellow or tan. If your bear is a different color, use a darker shade of the body color.

5

Paint fuzzy shadows

Dabbing in shadows with a brush or cotton swab will make your bear look fuzzy. Dip your small brush or swab in the dark paint from step 4 and dab it on newspaper first. Then dab the paint in the middle of the tummy and around the arms, legs and the head.

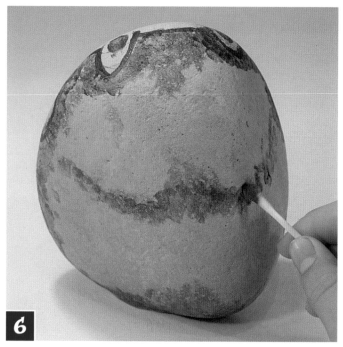

Paint the back

Turn the rock over and dab soft shadows at the bottom. Dab wing-shaped shoulder blades just above the center. Also add some shadows behind the ears.

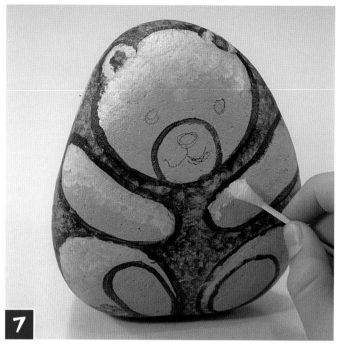

Add fuzzy highlights

Mix a tiny dot of your bear's main color with a drop of white paint. Use a clean, damp cotton swab or paintbrush to dot this color around the ears, the top of the head, the tops of the arms and the tops of the legs.

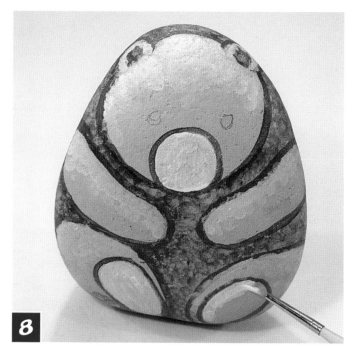

Paint the muzzle and feet

Use a small or medium brush and plain white paint to paint the muzzle and the bottoms of the feet.

Add black touches

Use your small brush and black paint to darken the shadows around the bottom edge of the head, the bottom edges of the front feet and between the legs. Then paint two small eyes, a small round nose and two curved mouth lines below the nose.

317

Paint the toes

Use black paint to add three small toe lines to each foot. If you like your bear, go to step 13, or you can follow the next steps to add furry details.

Add fur (optional)

To make your bear look furry, add a little water to the color you used in step 7. Use your smallest brush to add tiny lines around the head, ears, legs, and the tops and bottoms of the arms. Add these lines to the shadows on the back of the bear, too.

Add furry shadows (optional)

Rinse your brush and add a little water to the dark color you used in step 4. Make clusters of short brown lines on the bear's cheeks. Also add a row of lines along the bottoms of the arms and legs.

Paint eye highlight

A tiny dot of pure white off center in each black eye will make your bear seem to be looking back at you!

more ideas

Tiny bears make great gifts or party favors. Doll-size straw hats from a craft store come in different sizes to fit almost any rock bear.

319

The material in this compilation appeared in the following previously published North Light Books, and appears here by permission of the authors. (The initial page numbers given refer to pages in the original work; page numbers in parentheses refer to pages in this book.)

Wellford, Lin	Painting Zoo Animals on Rocks © 2003	Pages 1, 4–126 (5–130)
Wellford, Lin	Painting Pets on Rocks © 2000	Pages 1, 4–127 (131–257)
Wellford, Lin	Painting on Rocks for Kids © 2002	Pages 1, 4–63 (258–319)

Other fine North Light books are available from your local bookstore, craft store or direct from the publisher.

09 08 07 06 05 5 4 3 2 1

Painting Animals on Rocks / edited by North Light Books–1st ed.
          p. cm.
     ISBN 1-58180-735-X (hc.: alk. paper)

Cover Designer: Clare Finney
Production Editor: Jennifer Ziegler
Production Coordinator: Kristen Heller